C000219553

# INGIMUND'S ᴊᴀᴏᴀ. NORWEGIAN WIRRAL

## BY

## STEPHEN HARDING

*With Foreword by Magnus Magnusson K.B.E.*

Countyvise Publications, Wirral UK, 2000

In conjunction with:
The Borough of Wirral
The City of Trondheim
Braathens
Unilever Research, Port Sunlight

First published 2000 by Countyvise Limited,
14 Appin Road, Birkenhead, Merseyside, CH41 9HH

British Library Cataloguing in Publication Data.
A Catalogue record for this book is available from the British Library.

ISBN 1 871201 09 8

*To my Grandparents and other old Vikings everywhere*
*- this life and the next*

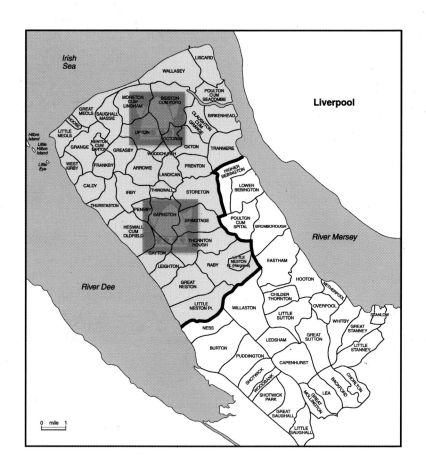

Irish
Sea

Liverpool

Hilbre
Island
Little
Hilbre
Island

Little
Eye

LISCARD

WALLASEY

POULTON
CUM
SEACOMBE

MORETON
CUM
LINGHAM

BIDSTON
CUM FORD

GREAT
MEOLS

SAUGHALL
MASSIE

CLAUGHTON
CUM
GRANGE

BIRKENHEAD

HOOSE

UPTON

BIDSTON

LITTLE
MEOLS

NEWTON
CUM
LARTON

OXTON

TRANMERE

GRANGE

GREASBY

WOODCHURCH

FRANKBY

ARROWE

PRENTON

HIGHER
BEBINGTON

WEST
KIRBY

LANDICAN

LOWER
BEBINGTON

CALDY

THINGWALL

STORETON

IRBY

POULTON
CUM
SPITAL

BROMBOROUGH

THURSTASTON

PENSBY

BARNSTON

BRIMSTAGE

River Mersey

HESWALL
CUM
OLDFIELD

THORNTON
HOUGH

GAYTON

EASTHAM

LEIGHTON

RABY

LITTLE
NESTON
Pt. (Hargrave)

HOOTON

NETHERPOOL

GREAT
NESTON

CHILDER
THORNTON

OVERPOOL

STANLOW

River Dee

LITTLE
NESTON Pt.

WILLASTON

LITTLE
SUTTON

WHITBY

GREAT
STANNEY

NESS

LEDSHAM

GREAT
SUTTON

LITTLE
STANNEY

BURTON

PUDDINGTON

CAPENHURST

CHORLTON

SHOTWICK

BACKFORD

WOODBANK

SHOTWICK
PARK

GREAT
MOLLINGTON

LEA

GREAT
SAUGHALL

LITTLE
SAUGHALL

0   mile   1

# Ingimund's Saga

## Foreword by Magnus Magnusson KBE

If there is one kind of person I like and admire above most others it is an amateur enthusiast, someone who has become passionately involved with a 'specialised subject' of his own choosing. I had the pleasure of meeting, and getting to know, 1,231 of them during the 25-year run of *Mastermind* on BBC TV; I only regret that Steve Harding never felt tempted to try to make it 1,232.

Professor Stephen Harding is a scientist. To be precise, he is the director of the National Centre for Molecular Hydrodynamics at the University of Nottingham. So what on earth is he doing, writing a book about the Norsemen in Wirral a thousand years ago? Is he a historian? No. Is he an authority on the Viking Age? No. He is an amateur enthusiast - and that, to me, is everything. What's more, along with his joint-authorship of *Wirral and its Viking Heritage*, he is rapidly making himself a figure who commands respect in academic Viking circles.

Ingimund's Saga: Norwegian Wirral is a delight for anyone interested in that extraordinary eruption of energy we know as the Viking Age, when people from Scandinavia came pouring out of their homelands to trade and to raid, to conquer and to settle, driven by a thirst for adventure and an insatiable curiosity about the world. They dominated much of Northern Europe for long periods. They brought to the British Isles vigorous new farming practices, vigorous new art forms, a vigorous new mercantile entrepreneurialism. They founded and developed great market towns like Jórvík (York) and Dublin.

But the British Isles were also a staging-post and a springboard for further adventures. They voyaged farther west than any Europeans had ever been before. They founded new and lasting colonies in the Faroes and Iceland, they explored and established settlements on the west coast of Greenland, and made land on the eastern littoral of North America — the ultimate outpost they called Vinland.

Meanwhile the Swedes had been pushing east, through Russia, founding city-states like Kiev and Novgorod, pioneering new trade routes down its formidable rivers and opening up the route to Asia to exploit the exotic markets of Persia and China. But that's another story.

The Wirral was never a fabled saga area like Constantinople (Istanbul) and its Varangian Guard. It did not attract the attention of the Icelandic saga-writers who used to be our main source of information for much of the Viking Age. But history has its byways as well as its highways, and more and more it is the intimate histories of *local* areas we rely upon to fill out the details of the sprawling, rumbustious, colourful canvas of the Viking Age.

Steve Harding has now given the Wirral its own saga. Like the saga-writers of old, he has resuscitated identifiable people from the musty archives of the past and placed them on stage, alive and vibrant, ordinary and extraordinary at the same time.

*Ingimund's Saga: Norwegian Wirral* is aimed, I think, primarily at Wirralonians. But it has resonances which should echo far further afield, now that the Vikings are at last being recognised as ancestors of whose heritage we can all feel extremely proud.

Magnus Magnusson KBE                    November 2000

# Preface

In May 1976 a rather green or unripe 20 year old undergraduate student from Wallasey, Wirral, was sitting in a College Library at an old University revising for his final examinations in Physics. Rather bored, he gazed around him onto the bookshelves and *Scandinavian England* by F.T. Wainwright caught his eye: to the student's astonishment seemingly the majority of the book was about the Wirral. The student had known from his younger days a bit about 'Thór's Stone' at Thurstaston, had learnt something from his grandfather about the Thing at Thingwall and a little about King Canute ordering the sea back at (as locals believe) Meols, but nothing like the extent that a huge chunk of the Wirral was virtually a Scandinavian state with a defined boundary, its own administration, leader, language and customs. No-one had told him about this! Nothing in his school training, nothing in the local libraries or other institutions. Presuming most of the Wirral also didn't know he decided something needed doing. The opportunity arose some years later when as a science lecturer at the University of Nottingham he came into contact with Judith Jesch, Reader in Viking Studies there, and then Paul Cavill, Research Fellow of the English Place-Names Society.

The result has been twofold: the scholarly text *Wirral and its Viking Heritage* by Cavill, Harding and Jesch published by the English Place-Names Society in 2000. That book also includes contributions from distinguished historians and place-name experts who have done a great deal to establish our understanding of the Wirral Norse movement: this roster of experts includes Frederick Threllfall Wainwright (1917-1961), John McNeal Dodgson (1928-1990), William Gershom Collingwood (1854-1932) and John D. Bu'Lock (1928 – 1996) together with local scholars Andrew Wawn and Simon Bean. The interested reader is very much encouraged to obtain it.

*Ingimund's Saga: Norwegian Wirral* has been written with very much the local Wirralonian in mind, and technical detail has been kept to a minimum – for this the reader needs to refer to the *Wirral and its Viking Heritage* book. It should also be of considerable value to natives from Norway, Iceland, Ireland, Denmark or Sweden interested in where some of their lost cousins ended up all those years ago. Indeed it should be of value to people interested in Vikings everywhere. Even the student of Association Football will find items of interest – Tranmere FC, English League Cup Finalists of the year 2000 carry the flag of an old Norwegian name.

Without the continuous encouragement and help of Judith Jesch and Paul Cavill, *Ingimund's Saga: Norwegian Wirral* would not have been possible. There is also a large group of others whom the author would like to acknowledge for their help with its production: David Griffiths, another exile from the Wirral and now Fellow and Tutor in Archaeology, Department of Continuing Education, University of Oxford; Chris Lewis, University of Nottingham, Division of Geography; Antonio da Cruz, University of Liverpool, Department of Geography; John Woodhouse and John Hodgson, John Rylands Library, University of Manchester; Miriam Bennett, Picton Reference Library, Liverpool; Jennifer Done, Wallasey Central Reference Library, Wirral; Kate Mason, Little Sutton Library, Wirral; Barbara Bogin, Irby Library, Wirral; Sarah Jane Farr and Rob Philpotts, Liverpool Museum; John Larson and Brigitt Lydik Clausen, Merseyside Conservation Centre; Jenny McRonald, Heswall Society, Wirral; Humphrey Smith and Mike Pill, Heswall Photographic Society, Wirral; Revd. Roger Clarke, St. Bridgets Church, West Kirby, Wirral; Patrick O'Brien, local historian, Little Sutton; Mel Roberts, local historian, Bromborough, Wirral; Susan Nicholson of the Bromborough Society, Wirral; Greg Dawson, local historian, Irby, Wirral; Frank Biddle, Pasture Road, Moreton, Wirral; Peter Miller, Dibbinsdale

Nature Reserve; Peter Young, Town Clerk, Lichfield City Council; Øyvind Stokke and Anne Ulset of the Royal Norwegian Embassy in London; Eyrún Hafsteinsdóttir and Jón Baldvinsson of the Icelandic Embassy in London; Stein Thue of Trondheim Kommune, Department of Cultural Affairs; Jens Fredrik von der Lippe, Trondheim Aktivum AS, Visitor and Convention Bureau; Ian Coles, Wirral Borough Council Tourism & Leisure Services; Heidi Lervold of Aune-Forlag, Trondheim; Kristín Bragadóttir and Örn Hrafnkelsson of Landsbókasafn Íslands - Háskólabókasafn, Reykjavík; Mike Rigby of Braathens; Angela Doyle & Keith Scott of Warrington Museum; Allan Alsbury, local historian, Higher Bebington, and, right at the end of the project, Gavin Hunter of Unilever Research Port Sunlight and the Wirral Society, who proved a mine of knowledge particularly about Bromborough. Jonathan and Keren Barbier, and also Jonathan Wild of the British Trees Internet Club were of great help with the identification of the willow tree from Piladall illustrated in chapter 10. A special thanks to the team at Countyvise for turning the idea for this whole project into a reality. The EEC Environmental Birds Directive gave permission for me to reproduce the crane-bird picture by Serge Nicolle. Sallie Payne of the Ordnance Survey provided permission to use the 1:25000 Ordnance Survey to show the border area at Raby/Hargrave. Professor Jan Ragnar Hagland, specialist in Old Norse at the Institute of Nordistikk og Litteraturvitenskap, Norges teknisk naturvitenskapelige universitet - NTNU, Trondheim, advised with regards the Norwegian Things.

Without the generous sponsorship of the following Ingimund's Saga: Norwegian Wirral would also not have been possible: the Metropolitan Borough of Wirral, the City of Trondheim, Braathens, Unilever Research Port Sunlight, Unitor (Oslo and Wallasey) and the Royal Norwegian Embassy. A special mention is appropriate to the archivists/staff at

Chester Record Office (now Chester & Cheshire Archives & Local Studies). Although J. Dodgson in the fourth part of his multi-part treatise "Place Names of Cheshire" identified virtually all the major and minor names of the Wirral and their origins, he specified the Ordnance Survey locations of only a small proportion. To generate most of the locations of the minor names of Chapters 6 and 7 the author had to retrace the steps of Dodgson in going through all the Tithe Maps and Apportionments, which were used alongside modern Ordnance Survey maps to pinpoint the locations – this required a great deal of help and patience particularly from Caroline Picco, Paul Newman, John Hopkins, Margaret Cole and Derek Joinson at the Record Office. Finally Magnus Magnusson painstakingly went through the manuscript, spotting and correcting many errors and correcting a (seriously!) outdated translation I presented to him on *The Saga of Háralðr.* Any inaccuracies in the present text are solely the responsibility of the author.

Steve Harding                    Nottingham, August 2000

*Steve.Harding@nottingham.ac.uk*

# Abbreviations and Pronunciation

## Abbreviations used:

| | |
|---|---|
| ON | Old Norse |
| OIr | Old Irish |
| ODan | Old Danish |
| OE | Old English |
| AD | anno domini |
| JRC | John Rylands Charter |
| pers.n. | personal name |

## Old Norse

The old language of Norway and the Norwegian Vikings.

## Pronunciation of Norse letters

j is pronounced as a y such as in young
v is pronounced as a w such as in will
ö is pronounced like the vowel in her or purr (ø in modern Norwegian)
æ is pronounced like the i in hike or mice
The accent above a vowel as in á, é, í, ó, ú and also ý means the vowel is long

The following additional characters are pronounced as in th:
Lower case form: ð, þ
Upper case form: Ð, Þ
ð, Ð is the "voiced" form of "th" as in "the"
þ, Þ is the "unvoiced" form of "th" as in "think"

# Contents

# Chapter 1
## INGIMUND'S SAGA

*"It is abundantly clear that in Wirral we are dealing with an alien population of mass-migration proportions and not with a few military conquerors who usurped the choicest sites".* Frederick Threlfall Wainwright, Historian (1917-1961)

2000AD – the start of the 3<sup>rd</sup> millenium. A remarkable year in the history of the Wirral with Tranmere Rovers football club reaching the final of a major competition - the English League Cup in front of 80,000 spectators at Wembley Stadium – for the first time.

1000AD – the start of the 2<sup>nd</sup> millenium. Also remarkable in Wirral's history, since by this time it was a well established Norwegian or Scandinavian colony with its own language known as Old Norse, its own government called the Thing (at *Þingvöllr* – Thingwall), its own port at *Melr* – Meols, and a border defined by *Rá-býr* – Raby - to the south and *Mikill-dalr* - now lower Dibbinsdale – and Storeton Hill to the East.

Although a thousand years seems a long time since this mass migration into the Wirral and settlement of it occurred, in terms of generations of people it is in fact fewer than forty. These peoples brought with them their legends (about *Valhöll* - Valhalla, *Þórr* – Thór - and the other *Æsir* or gods) and their stories, such as those which subsequently formed the basis of the famous Icelandic sagas. They had their own beauty spots (such as *Píll-dalr* or "Willow Valley" at Hargrave and Úfaldi's Green at what is now Birkenhead Park) and places for rock climbing, such as at the *Brekka* - The Breck - in Wallasey Village

1

and the *Klintir* - The Clints at what is now Brotherton Park in Bromborough, and probably even their own horse race-tracks (*Hesta-skeið* - Heskeths at Irby and Thornton Hough).

Tranmere – as *Trani-melr* - had been well established by then – and would have been founded shortly after the arrival of the first Norwegian settlers led by *Ingimundr* in 902AD. Tranmere is in fact a pure Norwegian construction and comes from the elements *trani* – crane, and *melr* – sandbank. The cranes were not of the sort found at the Cammell Laird Shipyard but of the bird type. So we have "crane sandbank", or "the sandbank frequented by crane birds", and the word

*Trani-melr* (Tranmere). Water painting of cranes near a sandbank by Serge Nicolle and reproduced with the permission of the EEC Environment/Nature directive

2

"trani" is still used in modern Scandinavian for birds of this type: *trane* in Norway and Denmark, and *trana* in Sweden. Also, one of the most famous 20th Century Norwegian politicians was Martin *Tranmæl* (1879-1967), a key player behind the Norwegian labour movement. The name Tranmere is, however, just one of **more than six hundred** place names in the Wirral which also have Scandinavian, and largely Norwegian, elements – it is fair to say that nowhere else in the UK is there such a density in such a small area.

The following is extracted from some old Irish annals called the "Three Fragments" which describe the arrival of the first group of Norwegians led by Ingimund (called Hingamund by the Irish) into the Wirral at the start of the 10th Century. These were people who had attempted to settle first in Ireland – probably Dublin - but were driven out by Caerbhall, leader of the Leinster Irish. Then they tried Anglesey, but were driven out of there too – then received permission from "Edelfrida, queen of the Saxons" (Æthelflæd, daughter of Alfred the Great) to settle in Wirral (landing probably at the old trading port of *Melr* – Meols or *Vestri Kirkjubýr* – West Kirby) where they were at last able to "drop anchor" and settle for good.


THE STORY OF INGIMUND

(from "Fragmenta Tria Annalium Hiberniæ", Bibliotheque Royale, Brussels, MS. 5301-5320, fo. 33a-fo. 34b).

We have related above, namely in the fourth year before us, of the expulsion of the Norse hosts from Ireland; through the fasting and praying of the holy man, namely Céle Dabhaill, for he was a saintly, devout man... The Norsemen, then, departed from Ireland as we have said and Hingamund was their leader, and where they went to was the island of

Britain[1]. The king of Britain at this time was the son of Cadell, son of Rhodri. The men of Britain[2] assembled against them, and they were driven by force from the territories of the men of Britain. Afterwards Hingamund came with his forces to Edelfrida queen of the Saxons, for her husband, that is Edelfrid, was that time in disease (let no one blame me although I have already mentioned the death of Edelfrid, and it was from the disease that Edelfrid died, but I did not wish to leave unwritten what the Norsemen did after going from Ireland). Now Hingamund was asking lands of the queen in which he would settle, and on which he would build huts and dwellings, for at this time he was weary of war. Then Edelfrida gave him lands near Chester, and he stayed there for a long time. The result of this was, when he saw the city full of wealth and the choice of land around it, he desired to possess them. Afterwards Hingamund came to the leaders of the Norsemen and the Danes; he made a great complaint in their presence, and he said that they were not well off without good lands, and that it was right for them all to seize Chester and to possess it with its wealth and its lands. Many great battles and wars arose on account of that. This is what he said: "Let us beseech and implore them first, and if we do not get them willingly in this way let us contest them by force". All the leaders of the Norsemen and the Danes agreed to do this. Hingimund then came to his house, with an assembly following him. Though they made this council a secret, the queen came to know of it. Therefore the queen collected large forces around her in every direction, and the city of Chester was filled with her hosts.

The armies of the Danes and Norsemen assembled towards Chester and, since they did not get their consent by beseeching or supplication, they proclaimed battle on a certain day. On that day they came to attack the city; there

---

[1] Island of Britain = Anglesey
[2] Britain = Wales. The Vikings called Wales *Bretland* "Land of the Brits"

was a large force with many freemen in the city awaiting them. When the forces who were in the city saw, from the wall of the city, the great armies of the Danes and Norsemen approaching them, they sent messengers to the king of the Saxons who was in a disease, and on the point of death at that time, to ask his advice and the advice of the queen. This was the advice they gave: to make battle near the city outside, and the gate of the city should be wide open, and to choose a body of horsemen, concealed on the inside, and those of the people of the city who should be stronger in the battle should flee back into the city as if in defeat, and when the greater number of the forces of the Norsemen came inside the gate of the city the force hidden yonder should close the gate after this band and not admit any more; capture those who came into the city and kill them all. This was all done accordingly, and complete slaughter was thus made of the Danes and Norsemen. Great, however, as was that slaughter, Norsemen did not abandon the city, for they were stubborn and vicious, but they all said that they would make many hurdles, and put posts into them, and pierce the wall under them. This was not delayed; the hurdles were made, and the forces were under them to pierce the wall, for they were eager to take the city to avenge their people.

Then the king (who was on the point of death) and the queen sent messengers to the Irishmen who were among the pagans (for there were many Irish among the pagans), to say to the Irishmen: "Life and health to you from the king of the Saxons, who is in disease, and from his queen, who has all authority over the Saxons, and they are certain that you are true and trusty friends to them. Therefore you should take their side; for they did not bestow any greater honour to a Saxon warrior or cleric than to each warrior and cleric who came to them from Ireland, because this inimical race of pagans is equally hostile to you also. It is right, then, for you, as you are trusty friends, to help them on this occasion." This was the same as if it was said to them: "We have come from faithful friends of yours to address you so that you ask the Danes what token of lands and treasures they would give to those who would betray the city to them. If they accept this, to bring them to swear to a place where it will be easy to kill them; and when they will be swearing by their swords and by their shields, as is their custom, they will lay aside all their missile weapons." They all did accordingly, and they put away their arms. And the reason why the Irishmen did this to the Danes was because they were less friends to them than to the Norsemen. Many of them were killed in this manner for large rocks and large beams were thrown down upon them; great numbers also [were killed] by darts and spears and by every other means for killing man.

But the other forces, the Norsemen, were under the hurdles piercing the walls. What the Saxons and the Irishmen who were among them did was to throw large rocks so that they destroyed the hurdles over them. What they did in the face of this was to place large posts under the hurdles. What the Saxons did was to put all the ale and water of the town in the cauldrons of the town, to boil them and pour them over those who were under the hurdles so that the skins were stripped from them. The answer which the Norsemen gave to this was to spread hides on the hurdles. What the Saxons did was to let loose on the attacking force all the beehives in the town, so that they could not move their legs or hands from the great numbers of bees stinging them. Afterwards they left the city and abandoned it. It was not long after that [before they came] to wage battle again. *Translation by the late Professor I.L. Foster, of Jesus College, Oxford.*

So here the saga of Ingimund tells of his departure from Ireland with his fellow band of Norsemen, an aborted attempt to land in Anglesey followed by his arrival in the Wirral in or soon after 902AD after securing an agreement with Æthelflæd, queen of the Mercian English. It tells of his subsequent restlessness and of continued attempts of the Wirral Norsemen – in conjunction with groups of Irish and Danes - to acquire by force Chester, ending with the ominous note "it was not long after that before they came to wage battle again". The Ingimund saga is not only beautifully preserved in the Irish annals but is also supported by Welsh Chronicles which in *Annales Cambriae* and *Brut y Tywysogion* record the aborted attempt to settle in Anglesey. Although there is no direct record of him by the Anglo Saxon Chroniclers – who were more preoccupied by the Danes in the east - they do record the refortification of Chester by Æthelflæd in 907AD, which would correspond well with the time of increasing restlessness by the growing population of Wirral Norwegians – and their Irish and Danish associates. Apart from the largely Danish led movements from the east, the Wirral settlement – recorded in Irish and Welsh annals – is the only Norse settlement into England which is documented as such in Medieval times.

## The Ingimund manuscripts

The transcripts describing the story of Ingimund have themselves had a fascinating history. The particular part of the Irish annals containing the Ingimund story became known as the *Three Fragments*, which themselves became lost. A vellum manuscript of unknown antiquity came into the possession of a certain "Dubhaltach" Duald MacFirbis who made a copy. This then came into the possession of a Nehemias MacEgan. Although that particular copy was also subsequently lost, another copy that had been made eventually came into the possession of a John O'Donovan who edited and published the story with the Irish Archaeological and Celtic Society in 1860. For the last 140 years it has been under the scrutiny of scholars worldwide, but the general consensus now is that, despite the fictional parts of some of the story, the essence of the Ingimund story must be true. It fits in exactly with all the Norse place names and name-elements in the major and minor names of the area, which include Irish names such as Irby (Old Norse: *Irá-býr* "settlement of the Irish"), Liscard (Old Irish: *lios na carraige* "hall on a rock") and Noctorum (Old Irish *cnocc-tírim* "hill that's dry"). The same element *cnocc* appears in "Kneckyn" which is now Caldy Hill. We know there were also Danes in the area from Denhall "Danes spring", from Old Norse *Danir*, "Danes". We even know the site where Ingimund must have addressed his fellow Norsemen and Danes about the attack on Chester, in his pursuit of further lands: "Let us beseech and implore them first, and if we do not get them willingly in this way let us contest them by force"; this would have been at Cross Hill in Thingwall at a meeting of the "Thing".

## Language of the Wirral Settlement

This was without any doubt Old Norwegian (Old Norse). This was aptly described by the place name expert Richard Coates who, in his recent (1997-8) article appearing in the *Journal of the English Place Names Society* about Liscard wrote: "The impact of Scandinavian on the [modern] local dialect, and especially microtoponymic, vocabulary, as analysed by Wainwright and Dodgson, leaves no doubt which was the conversational language". Contributions by F.T. Wainwright and J. McN. Dodgson can be found in the *Wirral and its Viking Heritage* book.

Cross-Hill: The site of the Thing at Thingwall, where Ingimund discussed with his fellow Norsemen plans for obtaining Chester. View is from the Reservoir side of Barnston Road

## The book

The rest of this book will look at the reasons why these ancestral Scandinavians left Norway, where, based on analysis of place names, in Wirral they settled, their religious beliefs both before and after settlement, their centre of Government (the *Thing*) and communication with the rest of the Norse community, and their pastimes and recreation (including horse racing, rock climbing and even a board game deriving from their long winter nights from back home). We identify all the places in the Wirral with Scandinavian and Irish elements, giving where possible the meaning and identifying their precise location in terms of ordnance survey coordinates: where this is not possible we provide a considered estimate.

We recount legends attributed to these people by common folklore – such as the great hammer (*Mjöllnir*) of Thór: Thór's Stone at Thurstaston, and King Canute's chair at Leasowe. One of the greatest battles in English-Norwegian history is widely believed to have taken place on Wirral soil: we recall the battle of Brunanburh at Bromborough in 937 AD where the locals no doubt would have assisted a large army of fellow Norsemen from other parts of the Scandinavian community.

We don't know what happened to Ingimund after his exploits recorded in the *Three Fragments*: who were his successors and where he was buried will remain forever a mystery. However, we do have records of a large number of other Norse men and women in the region: they are recorded in Cheshire records and the Domesday Book as moneyers and landowners, such as Asgaut (*Ásgautr*), lord of the manor at Hargrave. They left their mark also by giving their names to scores of places. It is clear from these that women such as Gunnhild (*Gunnhildr*) and Ragnhild (*Ragnhildr*) at Tranmere and Ingrid (*Ingríðr*) at Capenhurst played a highly prominent role in the Wirral-Norse community: we focus on Sigrid

(*Sigríðr*) whose "Half land" is beautifully preserved in an ancient Wallasey Charter.

We finish off by giving a list of further reading for the interested person to follow up and some interesting Web sites – for example, you can now play (on-line) the Viking Board game *hnefatafl* or "Tablut" – just like those ancestral Wirral Norsemen! But first we look at the reasons why these people left their homeland in the first place, and one prominent figure in Norwegian History appears to have a lot to answer for...

# Chapter 2
## HARALD HÁRFAGRI

*"...hann hafði þess heit streingt, at láta eigi skera hár sitt né kemba,*
*fyrr en hann væri einvaldskonúngr yfir Noregi: he had made a solemn*
*vow neither to cut nor comb his hair until he was king of all Norway".*
Snorri Sturluson. Icelandic saga writer (1179-1241)

A relevant question: why did the Norwegians leave their
homeland in the first place before their mass migration into
the Wirral? We know from the Ingimund story that at least the
first wave of settlers came to the Wirral via Ireland because of
a special arrangement with Æthelflæda, queen of the Mercians
- but why leave Norway? The question is specially pertinent to
those who have visited this northern land and witnessed just
how beautiful it is. The author has been lucky enough to have
visited there several times: the photograph over gives just a
glimpse.

One theory, that they were attracted to the Wirral by Tranmere
FC has been disproved since the football team weren't formed
until some 1000 years later. The real reason, or at least the
principal reason, appears to be *Haraldr Hárfagri* – Harald
Fine-Hair, or Harald Hårfagre in modern Norwegian – who
lived from about 860 to 936 AD: although now the name of an
aeroplane (see illustration on page 15) Harald Hárfagri was
arguably the most famous king of Norway. *Egil's Saga*,
believed to have been written by the Icelandic historian Snorri
Sturluson, writes of him thus:

*Haraldr son Hálfdanar svarta, hafði tekit arf eptir föður*
*sinn; hann hafði þess heit strengt, at láta eigi skera hár sitt*
*né kemba, fyrr en hann væri einvaldskonungr yfir Noregi,*

Lofoten Islands, Norway, during the Midnight Sun.
Photograph Courtesy of Heidi Lervold, Aune-Forlag, Trondheim

which reads: "Harald, son of Hálfdan the Black, had succeeded his father; he had made a solemn vow neither to cut nor comb his hair until he was king of all Norway". The story of Harald is also told in greater detail by Snorri in *Heimskringla* (History of the Kings of Norway). Harald Hárfagri's link with Ingimund is that it was Harald's actions which ultimately led to Ingimund and his followers to leave Norway for ever.

Prior to the middle of the 9th century Norway had been ruled by a number of regional kings with occasional interference from Denmark and Sweden. These districts or *fylker* in Norway included Hedemark, Agder, Ringerike, Gudbrandsdal, Hadeland, Toten, Raumarike. *Heimskringla* (meaning "Orb of the World") was written by Snorri in the period 1223-1235 and covers the histories of the kings of Norway from their mythical origins up to 1177. Sturluson based his great work on the sayings and writings of *Skalds* or court poets, whose responsibility was to pass on records and stories from generation to generation.

*Haraldr Hárfagri.* Now the name of an aeroplane with the Braathens Airline, but also the name of one of Norway's most famous kings, responsible for Ingimund's expulsion and eventual colonisation of Wirral

15

Harald (full name Harald Hálfdanarson - "Harald, son of Hálfdan") from Westfold (Vestfold - west of the Oslofjord) was the son of Hálfdan the Black (or "Blackhaired"), king of regions in south & central Norway. Harald was ten years old when he succeeded Hálfdan who died in an ice accident at Roeken at Randsfjord. Assisted by his uncle (*Guthormr*) he

*Snorri Sturluson* (1179-1241).
Drawing by Christian Krohg

proceeded to unite Norway after a succession of successful battles. The Hordaland woman *Gyða* also takes some responsibility for this unity. Snorri, in "The Saga of Harald Hárfagri" in *Heimskringla* wrote:

> King Harald sent his men to a girl called Gyða, a daughter of King Eirík of Hordaland, who was brought up as a foster-child in the house of a great *bóndi* (freeholder, freeborn proprietor) in Valders. The king wanted her for his concubine, for she was a remarkably handsome girl, but rather high-spirited. When the envoys came there, and delivered their message to the girl, she answered that she would not throw her maidenhood away on a king who had no greater kingdom to rule over than a few districts: "And I think it surprising," she said, "that no king here in Norway wants to make the whole country subject to him, in the same way as Gorm the Old did in Denmark, or Eirík at Uppsala." The envoys found her answer rather haughty, and asked what she thought would come from such a response; for Harald was such a mighty man that he was every bit a match for her. But although she had replied to their

message differently from what they wished, they saw no chance on this occasion of taking her with them against her will, so they prepared to leave. When they were ready, and people escorted them out, Gyða asked the envoys to tell King Harald that she would only agree to marry him when he, for her sake, had subjected to his dominion the whole of Norway and ruled that kingdom as freely and fully as King Eirík over the Swedish realm or King Gorm over Denmark. "For only then can he be called the king of a nation".

Harald responded by vowing never to cut his hair until that feat was accomplished....

... "I make this vow, with God as my witness, who made me, and rules over all things, that I shall never cut nor comb my hair until I have subjugated the whole of Norway, with all its tribute, taxes and domains; or die in the attempt.".....

The subduing of the whole of Norway he subsequently achieved in a series of battles and treaties, culminating in one final great battle at Hafrsfjörður (now Havsfjord, just west of Stavanger) which took place in or about 890AD. After this he became the supreme King of all Norway, expelling all those who refused to submit to his leadership. This, according to Icelandic historical tradition, led to the great exodus of Norwegians largely from the western parts, such as Bergen and Kristiansand, and the northern parts such as Trondheim and Trondelag. Snorri describes in the saga this great movement as follows:

After this battle King Harald met no opposition in Norway, for all his worst enemies had fallen. But some, and they were a great number, fled out of the country and thereby great uninhabited districts were peopled....

Modern Trondheim. Formerly *Niðarós*, Norwegian capital in Viking times. From this area or surrounding districts Ingimund possibly came. Photograph Courtesy of Heidi Lervold, Aune-Forlag, Trondheim

[After King Harald had subdued the whole land] he was at a feast in Møre, given by Earl Rögnvald one day. King Harald now went to the baths and had his hair dressed. Earl Rögnvald cut his hair, which had been uncut and uncombed for ten years. Hitherto the king had been called Harald Lúfa (Mop-Hair), but Earl Rögnvald now gave him a new nickname - Harald Hárfagri (Fine-Hair); and all who saw him agreed that it was most appropriate, for he had a truly magnificent head of hair.

Although the Norse Viking expeditions had started in the 8th century - and raids in Ireland from about 795 AD - the great exodus of peoples out of Norway is said to have followed the

Hárfagri unification of Norway from 890AD onwards which saw them move to other lands, many never to return. Whereas the Danes largely came into England along its eastern coast as an attempted military conquest, the Norwegians who were either expelled by Harald or who were just following a great thirst for adventure – a characteristic of these peoples - headed west, settling in the Orkneys, Shetland, Faroes and Iceland. From there some headed further west to Greenland and America (as recorded in the Vínland sagas). After passing northern Britain, a large number then headed south, some stopping at the Isle of Man, and many ending up in the newly founded Viking kingdom of Dublin. It was from here that Ingimund's men were also expelled some years after the initial departure from Norway, as recorded in the *Three Fragments*. The final major expulsion of Norsemen occurred soon after the Battle of Clontarf in 1014AD, which probably marked the last of the exodus of Norwegians into the Wirral and surrounding areas.

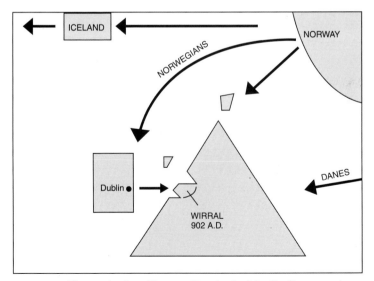

The exodus from Norway. Drawing by John Harding

# Chapter 3
## Six hundred Scandinavian places: a new Wirral-Norse "Mini-state"

*"They are incontrovertible proof that Scandinavians settled in great numbers in Wirral".* Frederick Threlfall Wainwright, Historian (1917-1961)

So having arrived in the Wirral in "mass migration numbers" from 902AD until 1014 or thereabouts, where did they all get to? More than 600 place names provide us with a clue as to how far they penetrated – and at what density. To assist, the illustration overleaf shows a 19th century map of Wirral parishes – a map which has remained little changed since the time of the Vikings and Domesday - and on it we have indicated the boundary or border demarking the limit of dense settlement: this border is essentially that suggested by the Wirral Archaeologist David Griffiths based on the distribution of major place names of Norse origin, and by J. Dodgson, based on Domesday baronial holdings of Norsemen. Parishes to the north and west of the border shown in the illustrations represent the main Norse enclave whose bounds are defined by the River Dee, Neston/Raby, Lower Dibbinsdale, Storeton Hill and Tranmere, the River Mersey and the the Irish Sea.

We can further test the accuracy of the border by looking at the distribution of **all** the names in Wirral – major and minor – of Scandinavian or Irish-Scandinavian origin. The minor names include field names and topographical features like hills and slopes (ON *brekka*, OIr *cnocc*), hillocks and mounds (ON *haugr*), hollows or "slacks" (ON *slakki*), projecting rocks (ON *klintir*), ravines or dips (ON *gil*), lanes or rakes (ON *rák*),

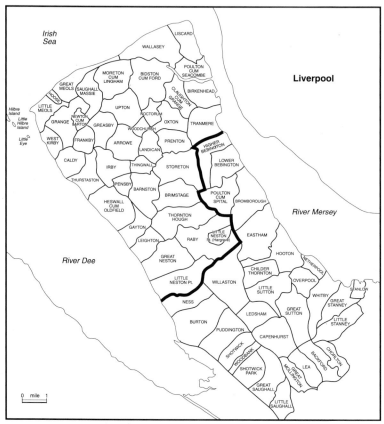

The Wirral Parishes and the Scandinavian enclave. The 19th century distribution of
parishes has remained remarkably unchanged since Viking times and Domesday.

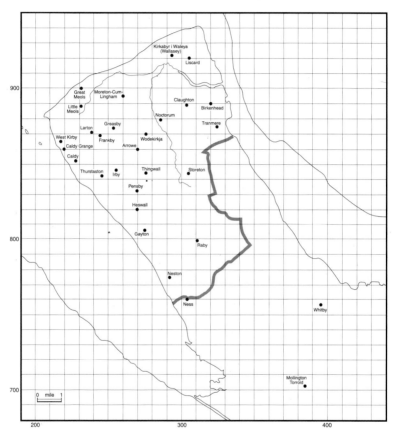

Major Wirral Place names with Norse elements

marshes or carrs (ON *kjarr*[3] ), and islands in marshy areas (ON *hólmr*).

To achieve this data, although earlier researchers such as J. McNeal Dodgson in his exhaustive treatise on the place names of Cheshire had identified the origins of virtually all of the place names in Wirral, their precise locations in terms of Ordnance Survey coordinates were provided for less than a few per cent. To pin down the other coordinates the present author spent many a day visiting the Chester Record Office to compare 19th Century Tithe maps and apportionments with modern day Ordnance Survey maps; visits to the John Rylands Library in Manchester, to view some of the ancient Wirral Charters now stored there, were also necessary. The result is illustrated below and demonstrates that indeed the Griffiths border – which had been suggested before this information was available – was indeed an accurate one although there is still clearly a large number of "outlier" settlements outside the main enclave. We can also see from this distribution how sensible was the choice by the settlers of a suitable place for the Thing: Thingwall is right in the centre of the Norse area.

Significantly the border cuts round the parish of Raby, a name which comes from the old Norse *rá-býr*[4] meaning "border village or settlement". Moving northwards from there it uses lower Dibbinsdale (or "Plymyard Dale"), Mickledale (from *Mikill-dalr* meaning "great-valley"), and then along the boundary between the north of Raby, Thornton, Brimstage and Storeton parishes with the "English" Poulton and Higher Bebington parishes – using the ridge of high ground, including what is now Prospect and Storeton Hills, up to "Norse" Tranmere parish as the Eastern extent. Raby, Hargrave/Little Neston and Neston parishes form the southern extent, with the old boundary probably not too far off from where Mill Lane and Damhead Lane now run.

---

[3] *kjarr* literally means "brushwood" of the type found in marshes, but for place names is generally taken as just "marsh"

[4] see note on page 27 about *býr* and *bær*

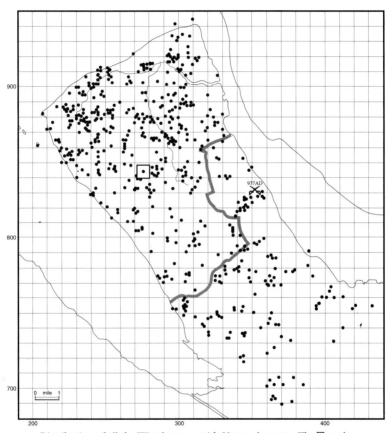

Distribution of all the Wirral names with Norse elements. The ⊡ marks
Þingvöllr (Thingwall). The battle sign marks the probable site
of the battle of Brunanburh, 937AD

The South Eastern border region covering the Raby, Hargrave and Willaston areas is covered in detail in Chapter 10. Hargrave itself, although an English name, was a Norse manor at least by the time of Domesday, with *Ásgautr*, recorded by the Domesday scribes as "Osgot", the pre-conquest lord. The English name for Hargrave ("the hoar wood" from OE har and græfe) also conveys a boundary. J. Dodgson, in Part IV of the Place Names of Cheshire writes on page 228:

Hargrave was a manor in the same hands as Little Neston. The element har is probably used here in the sense 'boundary' hence 'the boundary wood', cf. Raby. Boundary marks and territory would tend to be left undisturbed for fear of trespass, and an unbroken wood or an untouched boundary stone would grow mossy, venerable and 'hoary' with age.

#### Modern boundary almost the same as the old
It is also interesting to note that the current boundary for Wirral Metropolitan Borough also cuts along the southern edge of Raby and Hargrave, although the full extent of the modern cut across the Wirral is from west to east and excludes Leighton and Neston, whereas the old Norse boundary cuts south west to north east and includes Leighton and Neston but excludes Bebington, Bromborough and Eastham from the main Norse enclave.

#### Confidence in the old Wirral Norse boundary
We can therefore use the boundary mark for the main Norse enclave shown in the illustrations with some confidence although there is clearly a case also for the inclusion of Ness parish and parts of Bromborough. It is interesting that in the Storeton/Bebington/ Bromborough "border" area one encounters former place names like le Gremotehalland (1330,

ON *Griða-mót* – place of a meeting under a truce), Lathegestfeld (1412, ON *Leið-gestr*[5] – unwelcome guest) and le Dedemonnes Greue (1323 - dead man's wood).

## The bys, holms, carrs, inntaks, slacks and rakes

Of the 600+ places, a number of Norse elements are particularly common (as will be apparent as the next Chapters are read). These include **14 býr**[6] (townships/ settlements) **24 hólmr** (utilisable islands in/on marshy areas), **50 kjarr** (marshes - see page 24), **37 inntak** (enclosures), **11 slakki** (slacks, hollows, cut-throughs or shallow valleys) and **96 rák** (rakes, lanes). It would be intriguing also to examine how these are distributed. Of the 14 *býrs* (townships/settlements), besides the major places such as Frankby, Greasby, Irby, Wallasey (originally "Kirkjubýr í Waleya"), Pensby, Raby, West Kirby and Whitby there are six which no longer exist: Haby (in Barnston parish), Hesby/Eskeby (in Bidston), Warmby (in Heswall), Kiln Walby (in Overchurch/Upton), Stromby (in Thurstaston) and Syllaby (in Great Saughall). All, bar Whitby and Syllaby, are within the main Norwegian enclave. Of the býrs the origins of Irby and Frankby are particularly worthy of remark: Irby no doubt included some of the Irish who came with the Norsemen from Ireland. Frankby could well have been the home of a Frenchman (*Frankis-maðr*) although when and why he came we do not know: it has also been suggested that Frankby could have derived from the ON personal name *Frakki*. Irby is interesting for another reason. The distinguished Scandinavian Place Names expert Gillian Fellows Jensen believes that the route from Ireland was a facet rather than the cornerstone of the migration route of the Vikings into Wirral, and many came in fact via the Western Isles of Scotland, the

---

[5] Suggested by J. Dodgson. More recent interpretations have been "Visitor's guide" or "Visiting guide's" - see page 81

[6] In Old Icelandic the element *býr* became largely replaced by *bær*. For example, the place name *Vestri-Kirkjubær* in Iceland is exactly equivalent to the Wirral's *Vestri Kirkjubýr*, "The West Village of the Church", now the modern West Kirby.

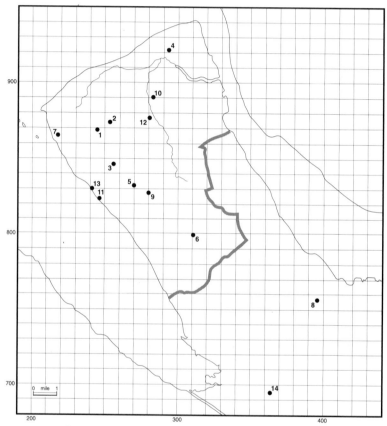

Distribution of the "bys". From Old Norse *býr* meaning "settlement".
1=Frankby, 2=Greasby, 3=Irby, 4=Kirby in Wallasey, 5=Pensby, 6=Raby,
7=West Kirby, 8=Whitby. The following no longer exist: 9=Haby,
10=Eskby/Hesby, 11=Warmby, 12=Kiln Walby, 13=Stromby, 14=Syllaby

Isle of Man and direct from Norway. Thus Irby could represent the settlement of Vikings who had come via Ireland implying the rest had arrived at the Wirral by some other route. Margaret Gelling has suggested that Ingimund and the first settlers became Viking overlords, facilitating the safe settlement of subsequent waves of Norse farmers.

### Wirral Marshes – carrs and holms

The bulk of the 50 or so *kjarr* (marshland) are concentrated in the north-west of the enclave (and all well within the border) and not surprisingly cluster around the flood plains of the River Birket and River Fender. This includes eleven places in Meols bearing this element, five each in the Moreton and Newton/Larton areas, ten in Saughall Massie, three each in Grange and Landican, two each in Oxton and Wallasey/Bidston (Bottom o'th carr's is the site for Wallasey Grammar School – now Wallasey School – at the eastern end of Birket Avenue) and one each in Hoylake, Pensby and Overchurch/Upton. The 24 hólmrs (islands of useable land within marshy areas) are also clustered around the Fender and Birket. Besides Lingham, five others are in the Moreton area, two in Claughton, four in Oxton, six in Prenton, and one each in Newton/Larton, Overchurch/Upton, Neston, Leighton, Great Stanney and Stanlow. Only the latter two lie outside the main enclave.

### Wirral farming enclosures – the inntak

The 37 *inntak* are somewhat less polarised into the main enclave. Inside the enclave there are 23 in total: Barnston parish (1 inntak) Bidston (1), Caldy (2), Claughton (1), Meols (1), Irby (2), Moreton cum Lingham (3), Neston (5), Pensby (1), Prenton (1), Storeton (1), Thingwall (1), Thornton (1), Tranmere (1) and Wallasey (1). Outside the main enclave there are 14 at Bromborough (1), Capenhurst (1), Ledsham (3), Stanlow (1), Whitby (4), Willaston (4).

## Wirral slacks or "hollows"

There are 12 place names bearing the element *slakki* of which interestingly the majority are distributed along the Dee side of the Wirral. Within the enclave there are five: of these, the Heswall Slack, which is now Milner Copse/ Milner Road appears to have received the most attention. It is a definite dip or hollow near Heswall Hill in the ridge of high ground running along the Eastern side of Wirral. Slack Road (now Milner Road) runs from here to Barnston. Just off the road a public house now known as the Sandon Arms was in former years itself called *The Slack* (see Chapter 6). The other four "enclave" entries for *slakki* are two at Raby (Slackey Field and Slack Hey) and one each at Tranmere (Slack Field) and West Kirby (Slack). There are six outside the enclave: three at Bromborough (Slack Wood in Brotherton Park, "The Slack" in what is now the north end of Eastham Country Park, and Acre Slack by the railway) and one each at Burton (Slack Lake and Field), Great Saughall (Slack Croft), Whitby (Byman's Slacks) and Woodbank (Slack Croft).

## The Wirral rakes

The rakes ("lanes") provide an even more interesting situation. There are an extraordinarily large number (96) in the Wirral and by far the largest density in the country. The ON root is the word *rák*, which literally means "stripe", adapted to refer to a lane or track. Rake can also derive from the English hraca, literally meaning a throat, neck, but does not occur in such a large frequency in other areas of the country.

The rakes are considered in some detail in *Wirral and its Viking Heritage* which provides an explanation for the large proliferation in Wirral: the existence of the Old Norse word in the Viking population and a similar word with similar meaning just across the border with the English led to the adoption of a cross-border pidgin word with a local meaning "lane".

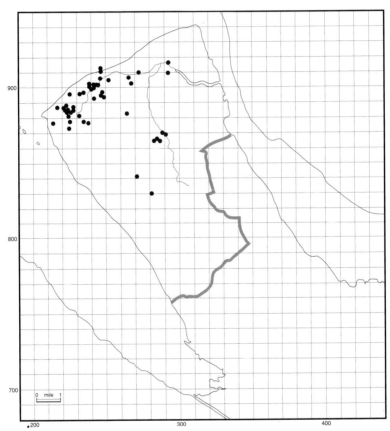

Distribution of the "carrs". From Old Norse *kjarr*, meaning "brushwood/marsh".
Note the heavy density around the Rivers Birket and Fender

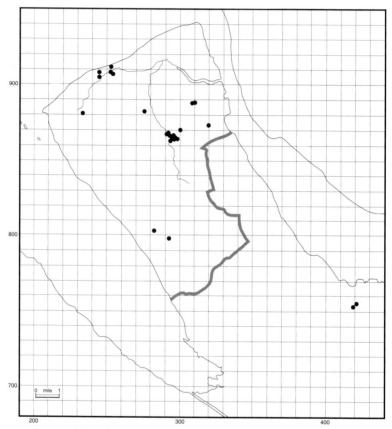

Distribution of the "hólms". From Old Norse *hólmr*, meaning "island of useable area
in a marsh". Note also the heavy density around the Rivers Birket and Fender

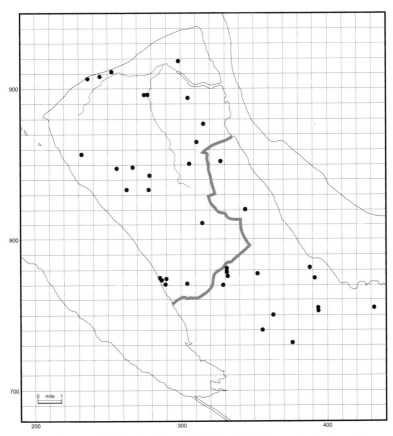

Distribution of the "intakes". From Old Norse *inntak*, meaning "enclosure"

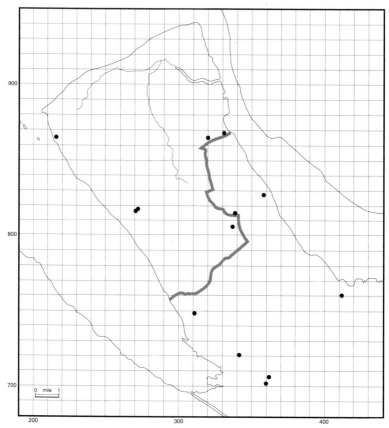

Distribution of the "slacks". From Old Norse *slakki*, meaning "a hollow". The most familiar is the Heswall Slack at SJ272818

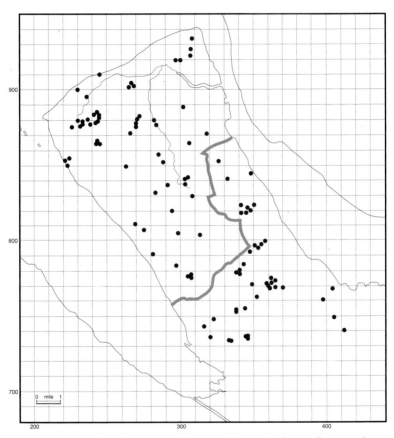

Distribution of the "rakes". From Old Norse *rák*, meaning lane, pathway, track.

**Wirral Norse mini-State Established**

So in a relatively short period of time a new independent, self-governing Norse "mini-state" was created with:

- a clearly defined border
- its own leader (*Ingimundr*)
- its own language (Norse)
- its trading port (Meols)
- and place of assembly or government (the Thing).

**This Norse mini-state - and its people - were answerable to nobody else: the English, the Welsh, the Dublin Norse, Isle of Man, Iceland - and especially not Hárfagri's Norway.**

We can now offer a glossary of all the places bearing Norse elements and their locations, both inside and outside the main enclave. For a more detailed and accurate description of the place name meanings the reader is referred to *Wirral and its Viking Heritage* and also Part IV of J. McNeal Dodgson's four part treatise on *The Place Names of Cheshire*.

# Chapter 4
## FOR THE ANORAKS

The following three chapters presents a complete list of Wirral locations of Norse origin.
- Major Viking Place Names
- Minor Viking names inside the Wirral-Norse enclave
- Minor Viking names outside the Wirral-Norse enclave

For the minor names we have grouped them by parish. The abbreviation ON means Old Norse (Old Norwegian), ODan: Old Danish, OIr: Old Irish, OE Old English, and pers.n. means "personal name".

Besides giving the Norse origins of each name, for the benefit of the "anorak" we have also given the precise location in terms of Ordnance Survey coordinates correct to 100m. So for example to find where the pool named after the Viking lady Gunnhildr, "*Gunnhildr's Pool*" in Tranmere parish used to be, the coordinates SJ330872 mean that in the Ordnance Survey sector SJ (all Wirral is in this sector) the easting is 330 and the northing is 872, or to find where the Vikings are believed to have raced their horses at *Hestaskeið* ("horse track", "horse race track": Heskeths) in Irby parish from SJ257844 means an easting of 257 and a northing of 844.

For the major places, if you are tracking these places a 1:50000 scale "Landranger" map will do. Unfortunately the Ordnance Survey people have split Wirral into two so it will be necessary to use two maps. For the minor places the 1:25000 scale Landranger maps will be necessary or the more detailed 1:10000 maps. Where there is some doubt about the precise location of some of those places which no longer exist (e.g. *Sigríðr's Halfland* in Wallasey) an asterisk * is placed against the coordinates. Where a place no longer exists, the latest year of its recording is given, e.g. *Le Rake* (1347) in the Barnston area.

For the minor places we have avoided – or tried to avoid – including those place names which, although carrying Scandinavian elements, are clearly modern in origin. So, for example, Gautby Road, running from SJ292902 to SJ297903 in the Bidston area with the ON elements *Gaukr, býr*, is ruled out. Others where there is serious doubt about the antiquity, such as Sven Tor at SJ258819 in the Heswall area, carrying the ON personal name *Sveinn*, have also been excluded, but there have doubtless been some errors in what we have and what we have not included. It has to be appreciated also that when the Scandinavians did settle in their large numbers in the area they did not necessarily alter or "Scandinavianize" the names of those places which had already been named. Place name experts - of which I am not one - occasionally disagree or modify their opinion on the origin of a particular place, as witnessed by the lively discussion in the *Journal of the English Place Names Society* run from the University of Nottingham. One recent example is Liscard which was shown in a recent (1997-8) article by R. Coates to be clearly Irish-Scandinavian in origin.

Of the large numbers of places listed in Chapters 5-7, the following are definitely worth visiting:

- Cross Hill (Thingwall) – the place of the Wirral Thing
- Thór's Stone at Thurstaston – *Mjöllnir* (Thór's hammer)
- The Breck at Wallasey Village – if you can, climb the Clynsse (klint) – the large rock, as the Vikings once did
- The sea front at Meols – stand there and imagine the first settlers arriving in their Viking ships at, or soon after, 902AD
- St. Bridgets Church, West Kirby – where the beautifully

restored hog-back tombstone of a once prominent Wirral Norse citizen resides

- Hestaskeið (Heskeths) in Irby and Thornton Hough – where the Vikings used to race their horses
- Piladall (Willow Valley) – an old Viking beauty spot, right on the boundary/border at the bottom end of Bromborough Golf course
- The hills at Storeton, and also the grounds of what used to be Bromborough Court House – both believed to be prominent sites in the 937AD Battle of Brunanburh
- Tranmere Rovers Football club – the latter day champions of *Tranimelr* and the Wirral Norse.

If you are visiting Birkenhead Park remember the old Viking *Úfaldi*, who was once in charge of this area; and if you are visiting the Riveacre Country Park at Hooton remember another one, *Ketill* – this area was once his. Other interesting places are given in Chapter 14, but it is worth adding here that if you just happen to be an Icelander reading this and either visiting – or planning to visit - Wirral then besides Thingwall and Meols – which is the same as your *Thingvellir* and *Melar*, make a point of also going to West Kirby – the same as your *Vestri-Kirkjubær*.

# Chapter 5
## THE MAJOR VIKING
## PLACE NAMES IN WIRRAL

For the enthusiast, to find these places a 1:50000 scale Landranger Ordnance Survey map is sufficient.

### ARROWE
SJ270860 "A shieling", from ON *erg*

### BIRKENHEAD
SJ320890 *Birki-höfuð* "Headland growing with birch trees", from ON *birki* and ON *höfuð*

### CALDY
SJ228852 *Kald-eyjar* "Cold-islands" from ON *kaldr* and ON *ey* or *eyjar* (plural). An early form given also has the element OE *ears* (instead of *ey*) – literally means "arse" or "backside"! However J. Dodgson provides a convincing argument that it derives from the old Caldy Hundred which had for its nucleus present Caldy, West Kirby and the Hilbre islands with the collective title "the district at the cold islands"

### CALDY GRANGE (NOW GRANGE)
SJ220860 "Cold-island Grange" from ON *kaldr* and ON *ey* or *eyjar*.

### CLAUGHTON
SJ304889 *Klakkr-tún* "Hamlet on a hillock" from ON *klakkr* (hillock) and ON *tún*, or OE *tun*

## FRANKBY

SJ245869 *Frankibýr* "Franki's (or Frakki's) village or settlement" from ODan pers.n. *Franki* or ON pers.n. *Frakki* and ON *býr*[7]

## GAYTON

SJ275806 *Geit-tún* "Goat farmstead", from ON *geit* and ON *tún*

## GREASBY

SJ254874. From ON *býr*. Scandinavianized form of OE *Gravesberie*

## GREAT MEOLS

SJ232900 "Great Sandbank" from ON *melr* (sandbank, sandhills)

## HELSBY

SJ490755 "*Hellis-býr*" Village at the cave or hole. Just outside Wirral but a Norse outlier. Helsby Hill can be clearly seen from the M56 motorway on the southern side.

## HESWALL

SJ270820 "Hazel spring" from ON *hesli* or OE *hæsel*, OE *wælla* (spring). Early forms rule out ON *hestur* (horse) and *völlr* (field)

## IRBY

SJ256846 *Íra-býr* "Settlement of the Irish", or possibly "Settlement of Scandinavians from Ireland", from ON *Íra* and ON *býr*

## KIRKJUBÝR Í WALEYA (NOW WALLASEY VILLAGE)

SJ294922 "Village of the Church in Wallasey" from ON kirkja, ON *í*, and ON *býr*

---

[7] See footnote on page 27 about *býr* and *bær*

## LARTON
SJ239871 *Leir-tún* "Clay farmstead" ON *leir*, ON *tún*

## LISCARD
SJ305920 "Hall at the rock" from OIr *lios na carraige*. Possibly influenced by ON *skarð* (scar/rock)

## LITTLE MEOLS
SJ232888 "Little Sandbank" from ON *melr* (sandbank, sandhills)

## MOLLINGTON TOROLD (NOW GT. MOLLINGTON)
SJ385703. From ON pers.n. *Þóraldr*

## MORETON-CUM-LINGHAM (NOW MORETON)
SJ260900 *Lyng-hólmr* "Heather island on a marsh" from ON *lyng*, ON *hólmr*

## NESS
SJ304760 *Nes* "Promintory" from ON *nes* or OE *næs*

## NESTON
SJ292775 *Nes-tún* "Farmstead at or near the promintory" from ON *nes* or OE *næs* and ON *tún* or OE *tun*

## NOCTORUM
SJ286879 *Cnocc-tírim* "Hill that's dry" or "Dry Hill" from OIr *cnocc* (hill) and OIr *tírim*

## PENSBY
SJ270832 "Village or settlement at a hill called Penn" from ON *býr*

## RABY
SJ311799 *Rá-býr*, "Village or settlement at a boundary" from ON *rá* and ON *býr*: Settlement at the Norse/English border

43

## STORETON
SJ305844 *Stor-tún* "The great farmstead" from ON *stór* and ON *tún*

## THINGWALL
SJ276844 *Þing-völlr*, "Assembly field", or "Assembly fields" From ON *þing* and ON *völlr*. Meeting place or parliament for the Norse community in the Wirral. First meeting in or shortly after 902AD.

## THURSTASTON
SJ246842 *Þorsteins-tún* "Þorstein's farmstead" from ON pers.n. *Þorsteinn* and ON *tún*

## TRANMERE
SJ325875 *Trani-melr*, "Cranes' sandbank" from ON *trani* and ON *melr*. Sandbank with the crane-birds

## WEST KIRBY
SJ218865 *Vestri-Kirkjubýr*, "The west village of the church" from ON *vestri*, ON *kirkja* (church) and ON *býr*. The "west" distinguishes it from the other Kirkjubýr in Wallasey

## WHITBY
SJ396757 "The white manor or village". From ON *býr* and possibly ON *hviti* (white).

## WODEKIRKJA (NOW WOODCHURCH)
SJ276870 "Wooden church" or "Church in a wood". From ON *kirkja*. Predecessor of what is now Holy Cross Church.

# Chapter 6
## MINOR VIKING NAMES INSIDE THE WIRRAL-NORSE ENCLAVE

For the enthusiast to find these places a 1:50000 scale Landranger Ordnance Survey map is sufficient, although the 1:25000 and 1:10000 maps are better! Where there is uncertainty about the precise location, an asterisk * is placed against the Ordnance Survey coordinates.

### ARROWE AREA

*ARROWE BROOK & ARROWE BROOK HOUSE*
SJ253883 & SJ262865 "Brook at the shieling" from ON *erg*

*ARROWE HILL*
SJ275873 "Hill at the shieling" from ON *erg*

*ARROWE BRIDGE*
SJ265868 "Bridge at the shieling" from ON *erg*

*YOUD'S & BENNET'S ARROWE*
SJ268855 "Youd's and Bennet's shieling" from ON *erg*

*BROWNS ARROWE, BITHELS ARROWE, HARRISONS ARROWE, WHARTONS ARROWE, WIDINGS ARROWE*
SJ264865, SJ263863, SJ263860, SJ262857 and SJ263861 "Brown's, Bithels, Harrisons, Whartons and Widings shielings" from ON *erg*

*RAKE LANE,*
SJ270877 to SJ272882 "Lane" from ON *rák*

## TOP RAKE FIELD
SJ266871 "Field at the top of the lane" from ON *rák*

## BARNSTON AREA

## HABY
SJ280827 *Há-býr* "High-settlement" from ON *hár* (high) and ON *býr*

## PENSBY LANE (1831), NOW PENSBY ROAD
SJ269819 to SJ272840 "Lane to the village at a hill called Penn" from ON *býr*

## GILLS LANE/ GHYLLS LANE
SJ274839 to SJ280836 "Lane to a dip or ravine" from ON *gil*. Near a definite ravine or steep dip at the junction with Thingwall Road (Fender Valley). See also Gills Field & Meadow in the Pensby area.

**INTAKE** SJ278833 *Inntak* "Enclosure" from ON *inntak*

## RAMSDALE
SJ296833 *Hrafns-dalr* "Valley of the raven" from ON *hrafn* or OE *hræfn* (raven) with ON *dalr* (valley)

## SMALL FLAT
SJ280832. From ON *flatr* (flat)

## LE RAKE (1347) SJ283832* "The lane" from ON *rák*

## SLACK ROAD
SJ282821 to SJ271817 "Road in the hollow" from ON *slakki*. Now Milner Road, which at Heswall becomes the "Heswall Slack": see entry there.

The "gil" or ravine at the end of Gill's Lane in Barnston

## BIDSTON AREA

### BEDESTONCARRE (AT 1306: NOW BIDSTON MOSS)
SJ293910 "Bidston marsh" from ON *kjarr* (marsh)

### HESBY/ ESKEBY
SJ283890 *Askr-býr,* "Farmstead at a place growing with ash-trees" from ON *askr* (ash trees) and ON *býr*

### HOOLERAKE
SJ286904 "Lane to a hollow" or "Sunken lane" from ON *rák*

### GRASS & LITTLE HOVEACRE
SJ278891 "Marsh by the bank of a stream" from ON *kjarr*

**WALLACRE**
SJ293917. From ON *kjarr* (marsh) and possibly OE *wælla* (spring)

**INTAKE MEADOW**
SJ275896 "Meadow enclosure" from ON *inntak* (enclosure)

**OXHOLME**
SJ276903 *Öxna-hólmr* "(Island on) a marsh where oxen can pasture" from ON *öx* (ox), ON *hólmr* (island or useful part of a marsh)

**THWAITE LANE**
SJ278914 "Lane to or near a clearing" from ON *þveit* (clearing)

**THE CORNHILL THWAITE, THE GREAT THWAITE, MARLED THWAITE, MEADOW THWAITE, SALT THWAITE, SPENCER'S THWAITE, TASSEY'S THWAITE, WHINNEY'S THWAITE**
SJ79913, SJ281912, SJ277914, SJ79915, SJ282916, SJ281916, SJ277915 and SJ277913, "The Cornhill, The Great, Marled, Meadow, Salt, Spencer's, Tassey's and Whinney's clearing" from ON *þveit* (clearing)

**INDERTHWAITE (1522)**
SJ277912 *Innar-þveit* "Inner clearing" from ON *innar*, ON *þveit*

**UTTERTHWAITE (1522)**
SJ282916 *Úttar-þveit* , "Outer clearing" from ON *úttar* or ON *utar*, ON *þveit*

**OLUCAR (1347)**
SJ295912* *Ölur-kjarr*, "Alder marsh" from ON *ölur*, ON *kjarr*

## CALTHORPE
SJ288887 *Karl-* (or *kald-*) *þorp*, "Karl's (or cold) settlement" from ON pers.n. *Karl* or ON *kaldur* (cold) and ON *þorp* (settlement)

## HOLMEGARTH
SJ289888 *Hólm-garðr*, "Marsh-island enclosure", or "Enclosure on a useful part of a marsh" from ON *hólmr*, ON *garðr*

## BOSCUS DE GRESCOW (1357)
SJ289893* *Grjót-skógr* , "Gravel wood" - possibly one of the present Woods on Bidston Hill (Park Wood, Silver Birch Wood and/or Taylor's Wood) -from ON *grjót*, ON *skógr*

### BLAKELEY AREA: SEE NESTON AREA

### BRIMSTAGE AREA

## RAKE ENDS
SJ294820 "Lane ends" from ON *rák*

## RAKE SHUTE
SJ308830 "Lane shute" from ON *rák*

## STORETON FIELD
SJ309832 "Field of the big farmstead" from ON *stór*, ON *tún*

### CALDY AREA

## KNECKYN (CALDY HILL)
SJ225856 From OIr *cnocc*[8] : the same element is used in Nocturum

---

[8] As identified by W. Fergusson Irvine - see Chapter 8. J. Dodgson suggests the old Welsh *cnyc* rather than the Old Irish *cnocc*. A similar name *Knukyn* is recorded in 1307-23 in Irby

### CALDY BLACKS
SJ220850 to SK230840. From ON *Kald-ey* or *Kald-eyjar* (cold island/islands) A reef and bank off Caldy.

### THOR'S WOOD
SJ231855. From ON *Þórr*. Antiquity unknown

### INTAKE (FURTHER, HIGHER, MIDDLE, NEW)
SJ232856 *Inntak* "Enclosure" from ON *inntak*

### THE RAKE
SJ222854 to SJ224855 "The lane" from ON *rák*

### RAKE HAY
SJ223850 "Enclosure by the lane" from ON *rák*

### HINDOLTONS HAY
SJ232858 "Enclosure at the back of the farmstead" from ON *hindri* (back/rear)

### FURTHER INTAKE
SJ232856 "Further enclosure" from ON *inntak*

### MELLONS
SJ222850 to SJ219853 "Narrow strips of land" from ON *mjór*

### LOWER CALDY HAY, GREAT CALDY HAY
SJ238842, SJ230848. From ON *kald-ey* or *kald-eyjar*

### ASCOW (1454)
SJ234845* *Askr-skógr* "ash wood" from ON *askr* (ash), ON *skógr* (wood)

## SOUTERY LONDE (1454)

SJ230845* "The tanner's land" from ON *sútari* (tanner)

## THE BRANKERS PYTTE (1454)

SJ234858* *Brende-kjarr* "the pit at the burnt-out marsh" from ON *brent* (burnt), ON *kjarr* (marsh)

Caldy Hill, considered as the site of The Kneckyn

## THE KYRKE CROSS (1454)

SJ226852* *Kirkja-kross* "Church cross" or "A cross on the way to the church" from ON *kirkja* (church), ON *kross*. The "church" referred to is probably St. Bridgets at West Kirby.

## THURSTANTON WAY (1454)

SJ237856 to SJ245843 "Thorsteinn's way" or "Way to Thorsteinn's farmstead" from ON pers.n. *Þorsteinn*

## THE WRANGLANDES, WRANGOL (1454)

SJ226855* "Crooked selions" from ON *vrangr, rangr* (crook)

## THE WRO (1454)

SJ224855* "The corner" from ON *vrá, rá*

## CLAUGHTON CUM GRANGE AREA

## FLAYBRICK HILL

SJ293895 *Flaga-brekka* "Hill/slope with a flagstone" from ON *flaga* (flagstone), ON *brekka* (hill/slope)

## THE TASKAR (1546)

SJ297895 "The wood on which a toll or tax is levied" from ON *skógr* and possibly ON *tollr* (toll). The site of this is now on Bidston Avenue opposite Alderney Avenue.

## LOWER FLAT, FURTHER FLAT

SJ305889 and SJ306888. From ON *flatr* (flat)

## GILL FIELD, LITTLE GILL FIELD, GILL FIELD MOSS

SJ320895, SJ302900 and SJ304900 "Field in a dip/ ravine" from ON *gil*

**GILL BROOK**
SJ298896 to SJ305902 "Brook in a dip/ravine" from ON *gil*. Lost stream running in a dip/ravine. Now the name of a housing estate

**GILL BROOK BASIN**
SJ305902. From ON *gil*. An inlet in the docks at the mouth of the above lost stream

**LINGDALE (& HILL)**
SJ298887 *Lyng-dalr* "Heather-valley" from ON *lyng* (heather), ON *dalr* (valley)

**WINTHROP**
SJ294884 *Vindr-þorp* "Windy settlement" from ON *vindr* (wind), ON *þorp* (settlement)

**HOWBECK (ROAD)**
SJ296885 to SJ301886 *Haugr-bekkr* "Hillock/Barrow stream" from ON *haugr* (hillock, burial mound/barrow), ON *bekkr* (stream). Hillock is possibly site of the now Wirral Ladies Golf Course

**NEAR HOLMES WOOD, FURTHER HOLMES WOOD (1824)**
SJ310888 and SJ309888 "Near/Further marsh-island wood" from ON *hólmr*

**SEALS (1824)**
SJ309890 "Willow" from ON *selja*

**TOP, LOWER, FURTHER FLAT (1824)**
SJ302889, SJ303892, SJ304890. From ON *flatr* (flat)

## FLAT COW MEADOW (1824)
SJ295891. From ON *flatr* (flat)

## INTAKE (1824)
SJ305894 "Enclosure" from ON *inntak*

## VFELDESGRENE (1340)
SJ305890 "Úfaldi's green or wood" from ON pers.n. *Úfaldi*. Probably part of what is now Birkenhead Park

### FRANKBY AREA

## HILLBARK, HILLBARK FARM
SJ245857, SJ249858 "Hill cliff" or "cliff in a hill – alluding to a quarry face" from ON *bjarg*

## BIRCH HEY
SJ240863 "Birch enclosure" from ON *birki* (birch)

## LARTON HAY, LARTON HEY FARM
SJ237872, SJ238871 "Clay-farm enclosure" from ON *leir* (clay), ON *tún*

## TORPENHOW
SJ241860 *Þorp-haugr* "Settlement on a mound/hillock" from ON *þorp* (settlement), ON *haugr* (hillock, burial mound)

## SECOND RAKE HAY, NEAR RAKE HAY, GARDEN RAKE HAY, RAKE HAY BROW
SJ245864, SJ244865, SJ243864, SJ243865 from ON *rák*

## GAYTON AREA - SEE HESWALL AREA

## GRANGE AREA

### *LONG RAKE LANE (NOW HERON ROAD)*
SJ236895 to SJ245882 "Long lane" from ON *rák*

### *CARR*
SJ232881 and SJ224884 "Marsh" from ON *kjarr*

### *CARR FARM*
SJ242893 "Marsh farm" from ON *kjarr*

### *CARR FIELD*
SJ226878 "Marsh field" from ON *kjarr*

### *LARTON HAY, NEW LARTON HAY*
SJ239871, SJ232870 "Clay-farm enclosure" from ON *leir*, ON *tún*

### *MECCA BROOK*
SJ230881 "Gentle stream" from ON *mjúkr* (gentle, mild)

### *WYHON FLATT*
SJ235885* from ON *flatr* (flat). Adjoins the Flatts in Newton

### *GREASBY BROOK*
SJ247879 to SJ252846. From ON *býr*

### *RAKE HOUSE (AT 1847)*
SJ233877. From ON *rák* (lane)

### *RAKE HOUSE FARM, LONG RAKE FARM, RAKE FIELD, RAKE END*
SJ243878, SJ232876, SJ244885, SJ226875. From ON *rák* (lane)

## RAKE HAY (1639) FURTHER RAKE HEY (1780), LITTLE RAKE HEY, MIDDLE RAKE HEY, RAKE HEY MEADOW

SJ243883*, SJ230879*, SJ241883*, SJ237880*, SJ239877*. From ON *rák*

## SCAMBLANTS

SJ227878 "short selions" from ON *skammr* (short)

### GREASBY AREA

## BROAD FLATT, LITTLE FLATT, LONG FLATT, FLATTS

SJ255880, SJ252883, SJ255881, SJ253870. From ON *flatr* (flat)

## KIRKEWAY (1639)

SJ255873 to SJ245867 "Church way" or "the way to Church". (Not the modern Kirkway) from ON *kirkja*

## KIRKA LOONS, TOP KIRKA LOONS

SJ250871, SJ249872 "Church selions" from ON *kirkja*

## WIMBRICKS

SJ247879 *Hvin-brekka* "Gorsey slope on a hill" or "Gorse bank" from ON *hvin* (gorse), ON *brekka* (hill/ slope)

### GREAT MEOLS AREA

## CALDEY HAY

SJ234896 "Cold island enclosure" from ON *kaldur*, ON *ey* or *eyjar*

## INTAKE

SJ237907 *Inntak* "Enclosure", from ON *inntak*

### CARR SIDE FIELD, CARR HALL FARM, CARR FARM, CARR HOUSE

SJ232896, SJ245895, SJ242893, SJ248897. From ON *kjarr* (marsh)

### CARR LANE

SJ244902 to SJ249894. From ON *kjarr* (marsh)

## GREAT NESTON AREA – SEE NESTON AREA

## HARGRAVE/HARGREAVE AREA: SEE NESTON AREA

## HESWALL & GAYTON AREA

### SCARBROOK HILL ·

SJ265817 From ON *skarð*. Name (no longer used) for the hill up what is now Delavor Road

### SCARBROOK

SJ260817 to SJ254813 "Brook at a bluff or scar" from ON *skarð*. Brook which once ran down Scarbook Hill before the construction of culvert

### THE SLACK

SJ272818 *Slakki* "The hollow". Now Milner Copse & the site of the public house called Sandon Arms – formally "The Slack". From ON *slakki* (a hollow)

### SLACK ROAD (NOW MILNER ROAD)

SJ271817 to SJ282821. From ON *slakki* (a hollow)

**WALL RAKE**
SJ269811 "Lane by a well" or "Lane by a field" from ON *rák* (lane) with OE *wælla* (well) or ON *völlr* (field)

**RAKE DITCH**
SJ275807. From ON *rák*

**WARMBY (1831)**
SJ247823 *Varmr-býr* "Warm settlement" from ON *varmr*, ON *býr*

**WARMBY LANE (1831) (NOW BROAD LANE EXTENSION)**
SJ251821. From ON *varmr*, ON *býr*

**STACK YARD(S)**
SJ256830 and SJ265811 "Stack or pile yard/ Pillar yard" from ON *stakkr* (stack/ pile)

**TOWN FLATT, LOWER FLATT**
SJ272805, SJ271805. From ON *flatr* (flat)

**HARROWE HAY (1293)**
SJ266825* *Haerri-haugr* "The higher hill enclosure" from ON *haerri* (higher), ON *haugr* (hillock, burial mound)[9] . OE *hearg* "heathen shrine" has also been suggested.

### HILBRE & DEE ESTUARY AREA

**TANSKEY ROCKS**
SJ204860 *Tönn-sker* "Tooth skerry rocks" from ON *tönn* (tooth), ON sker (skerry)

---

[9] These elements together with ON *býr* form the name *Harrowby*, a now defunct West Cheshire League football team which at one time played at Meols/Hoylake.

The Heswall Slack or "hollow" (top), now Milner Copse/
Milner Road and (bottom) the Sandford Arms, formally "The Slack"

## HOYLAKE AREA

### CARR LANE
SJ217887 to SJ224885. From ON *kjarr* (marsh)

### ARNOLDS EYE (1819)
SJ207882 "Arnald's sandbank" from ON *eyrr* (a sandbank). Represents the northerly end of the Dee estuary on the Wirral side. The corresponding element appears in the name Point of Ayr at the end of the Dee estuary on the Welsh side. Could also be ON *eyjar* (islands).

## IRBY AREA

### IRBY HILL
SJ254861. From ON *Íra* (Irish), *býr* (settlement)

### HESKETHS
SJ257844 *Hesta-skeið*, "Horse track", Horce race-track" from ON *hestur* (horse), ON *skeið* (track). See Chapter 14.

### INTAKE MEADOW, YOUNG'S INTAKE
SJ256847, SJ267848. From ON *inntak* (enclosure)

### MICKANSEDGE
SJ253849 "Large brook" from ON *mikill* (great, large)

### RAKE HEY
SJ263849. From ON *rák* (lane) "Enclosure by the lane"

## LANDICAN AREA

### *CARREMEDOWE (CARR BRIDGE MEADOW)*
SJ287865 "Marsh Meadow" from ON *kjarr*

### *CARR BRIDGE FIELD, NEAR CARR BRIDGE FIELD*
SJ285866, SJ283865 "Marsh bridge field" from ON *kjarr*

### *STORETON FIELD HEY, FAR STORETON FIELD HEY*
SJ291853, SJ291851 "Enclosure by the great farmstead" from ON *stór*, ON *tún*

### *RAKES, RAKE SHOOTS*
SJ288852, SJ285857. From ON *rák* (lane)

## LEIGHTON AREA

### *HOMES HAYS*
SJ282803 "Marsh-island enclosure" from ON *hólmr* (marsh-island, or useable part of a marshy area)

### *RABY YATE (1569)*
SJ292800 *Rá-býr* gata ,"Street/ gate leading to Raby" from ON *rá* (boundary), *být* (settlement), ON *gata* (street) or OE *geat*

### *LE RAKE (1280)*
SJ281791* "The Lane" from ON *rák*

### *FLAT*
SJ291778 from ON *flatr* (flat)

## LISCARD AREA

### SWARTESKERE (NOW FORT PERCH ROCK, BLACK ROCK)
SJ310945 *Svart-sker*, "Black skerry" from ON *svartr* (black), ON *sker* (skerry)

### BRECK HEY
SJ297917 "Hill-side enclosure" from ON *brekka* (hill/ slope)

### BRECK ROAD
SJ296919 to SJ303915 "Hill-side road" from ON *brekka* (hill/slope)

### RAKE LANE
SJ307923 to SJ308934 from ON *rák* "lane"

### RAKE HEY
SJ307927 "Enclosure by the lane" from ON *rák*

### CAMBRICK HEY
SJ314920 *Kambr-brekka* "Enclosure at the ridge at the hill" from ON *kambr* (ridge), ON *brekka* (hill/ slope)

### LONG GOLACRE, FURTHER GOLACRE
SJ312919, SJ313918 *Góligr-akr* "Fair/Pretty-field" from ON *góligr, gólegur* (fair/pretty), ON *akr* (field, acre)

### STONEBARK (NOW STONEBY DRIVE)
SJ300933 to SJ303935 "Stoney cliff" from ON *bjarg* (cliff). See also entry for Wallasey area

### LE GATEBUT (1398)
SJ307920* "Street" from ON *gata*

## THE SHAMBROOKS (1654)

SJ310915* "Narrow brook fields" from ON *skammr* (narrow/short). Possibly the site of what is now Central Park

### LITTLE MEOLS AREA

## CARR

SJ228887 and SJ223885. From ON *kjarr* (marsh)

## CARR LANE FIELD

SJ225896 "Marsh-lane field" from ON *kjarr*

## CARR FIELD

SJ223888 "Marsh field" from ON *kjarr*

## CARR SIDE HEY

SJ222887 "Marsh side enclosure" from ON *kjarr*

## CARR HEY

SJ223888 "Enclosure at a marsh" from ON *kjarr*

## TORWOOD LEE

SJ234896, "Thór's wood" from ON pers.n. *Þórr*. Antiquity not known

### LITTLE NESTON AREA: SEE NESTON AREA

### MORETON CUM LINGHAM AREA

## LINGHAM

SJ252910 *Lyng-hólmr* or *Lang-hólmr*, "Heather-marsh island" or "Long marsh island" from ON *lyng* (heather) or ON *langr* (long), ON *hólmr* (marsh island, or useable area in a marsh)

### DANGKERS (NOW DANGER) LANE

SJ266907 to SJ268903 "Marsh lane" from ON *kjarr* (marsh)

### BOTTOM O' TH' CARRS

SJ273910 "Bottom of the marshes" from ON *kjarr*. Now the site of Wallasey School (formerly Wallasey Grammar School).

### WEST CAR, WEST CARR MEADOW, WEST CARR HAY

SJ247911, SJ247913, SJ252905 "West marsh" from ON *kjarr*

### HOLME HAY, BIG HOLME HAY, LITTLE HOLME HAY

SJ245905, SJ252908, SJ254907 "Marsh-island enclosure", or "Useable enclosure on a marsh" from ON *hólmr*

### HOLME ITCH

SJ245908 *Hólmr-inntak* "Marsh-island enclosure"

### LITTLE HOLME HAY, BIG HOLME HAY

SJ254907, SJ252908 "Little marsh-island enclosure", "Big marsh-island enclosure" from ON *hólmr*

### LINGHAM LANE

SJ252913 to SJ255903 "Heather-marsh island lane" from ON *lyng* (heather), *hólmr* (island)

### HOLME INTAKE

SJ253911 "Marsh-island enclosure" from ON *hólmr*, ON *inntak*

### INTAKE

SJ277896 *Inntak* "Enclosure" from ON *inntak*. At what is now the M53 Motorway interchange

### RAKE HEY

SJ265902 and SJ267904 "Enclosure by the lane" from ON *rák*

## RAKES MEADOW
SJ245911 "Lane meadow" or "Meadow Lane" from ON *rák*

## NESTON (GREAT & LITTLE) AREA

### STONE STUPES
SJ211766 "Stone post or pillar" from ON *stólpi* (post/pillar)

### HOLMES HEYS
SJ292798 "Marsh-island enclosures" from ON *hólmr* (island, useable part of a marshy area)

### RABY ROAD
SJ305791 to SJ310798. From ON *rá* (boundary) and ON *býr* (settlement). Antiquity uncertain

### RABY RAKE
SJ297783 *Rá-býr rák* "Lane to/from the boundary settlement", from ON *rá-býr* (boundary-settlement), ON *rák*

### RAKE ENDS, RAKE END CROFT, RAKE END ENCLOSURE
SJ305776, SJ307776, SJ307777. From ON *rák* (lane)

### THE INNTACK
SJ286774 *Inntak* "The enclosure" from ON *inntak*

### INTACK
SJ290774, SJ289771, SJ287773, SJ304771 *Inntak* "Enclosure" from ON *inntak*

### SOUR FLATT, FLATT HEATH
SJ298797, SJ316782. From ON *flatr* (flat)

## BLAKELEY/ HARGRAVE DISTRICT OF LITTLE NESTON PARISH

**PILADALL**
SJ343798 to SJ338796 *Píll-dalr* "Willow valley" from ON *píll* (willow), ON *dalr* (valley). See also entries for Pellerdale in the listings for Raby area, and also Piledale (Willaston area, Chapter 7)

**MICKLEDALE (now PLYMYARD DALE)**
SJ340818 to SJ342789 *Mikill-dalr* "Great-valley" from ON *mikill* (great, large), ON *dalr* (valley). Connects with Willaston parish (Chapter 7)

**MICKLE MOOR MEADOW (1711)**
SJ337802 "Large moor meadow" from ON *mikill* (great, large).

### NEWTON CUM LARTON

**FORNALL (BRIDGE & GREEN)**
SJ235895 to SJ235895 *Forn-haugr* "Old mound/hillock" from ON *forn* (old), ON *haugr* (hillock, burial mound)

**NEWTON BREKEN**
SJ238875 "Newton slope/ hillside" from ON *brekka* (hill, slope)

**LARTON HEY FARM**
SJ23987. From ON *leir* (clay), ON *tún* (farmstead)

**NEWTON CAR (AT 1842)**
SJ225881. From ON *kjarr* (marsh)

**SALLY CARR LANE (now footpath)**
SJ235878 to SJ238877 *Selja-kjarr* "Lane at Willow Marsh" from ON *selja* (willow), *kjarr* (marsh)

**CARR LANE**
SJ214877 to SJ225873 "Marsh lane" from ON *kjarr*

**CARR, CARR MEADOW**
SJ228885, SJ226884. From ON *kjarr*

**HOLMESIDES**
SJ234881. From ON *hólmr*

**NEAR FLATT, FAR FLATT, SAWGHON FLAT, GREAT FLAT, LITTLE FLAT**
SJ225873, SJ236873, SJ232882, SJ235877, SJ235883. From ON *flatr* (flat)

**BANAKERS**
SJ236877. From ON *akr* (field, acre) or ON *kjarr* (marsh)

**NEWTON RAKE, RAKE HOUSE, LONG RAKE FARM**
SJ244879*, SJ233878, SJ233877. From ON *rák* (lane)

## NOCTORUM AREA

**SHIRBECK**
SJ291881. From ON *bekkr* (stream)

**RAKE HEY, BIG RAKE HEY**
SJ282879, SJ288876. From ON *rák* (lane)

**FLAT**
SJ288876. From ON *flatr* (flat)

## OVERCHURCH/UPTON AREA

### *KILN WALBY (GILDEWALLEBY), TOP KILN WALBY, KILN WALBY MEADOW, LOWER KILN WALBY*

SJ281877, SJ275868, SJ281880, SJ279880 *Gildi-býr* "Guildsman's settlement", "Settlement at the Guildsman's spring" from ON *gildi* (guildsman), ON *býr* (settlement). Also OE *wælla* (spring)

### *KILL FLATT (1666)*

SJ277879* *Gildi-flatr* "Guildsman's flat (land)" from ON *gildi*, ON *flatr*

### *GREASBY FLAT*

SJ254885. From ON *býr* (settlement), ON *flatr* (flat)

### *MORETON FLATT*

SJ256888. From ON *flatr* (flat)

### *FLATTS*

SJ252885. From ON *flatr* (flat)

### *SALACRES*

SJ273879 *Selja-akr* or *Selja-kjarr* "Willow field" or "Willow marsh" from ON *selja* and ON *akr* or ON *kjarr*

### *SALACRE LANE*

SJ272881 to SJ276877. From ON *selja* and ON *akr* or ON *kjarr*

### *LANACRE*

SJ266885. From ON *akr* (field, acre) or ON *kjarr* (marsh)

### *RAKE LANE*

SJ270876 to SJ271881 from ON *rák* (lane)

## HOUGH HOLMES
SJ276882. From ON *hólmr* (island, useable part of a marshy area)

## LE KAR (1294)
SJ265883 "The marsh" from ON *kjarr*

## OVERKIRK HILL
SJ269886 from ON *kirkja* (church). Now the site of Overchurch school

### OXTON AREA

## ARNEHOW (NOW ARNO HILL, THE ARNO)
SJ306871 *Árni-haugr* "Árni's hillock/ burial mound" from ON pers.n. *Árni*, ON *haugr* (hillock, burial mound)

*Árni's* Hill - Arno Hill in Oxton. Is *Árni* buried here?

69

**SPATH, LITTLE SPATH**

SJ302874, SJ302873. From ON *sporðr* (fish-tail)

**CROOK LOON**

SJ301875 "Crooked loon" from ON *krókr* (crook)

**HOLM LANE**

SJ296866 to SJ320873. From ON *hólmr* (marsh-island, useable part of a marshy area)

**NEW HOME (1831), HOME FIELD, HOME HEY, LITTLE HOME**

SJ300870\*, SJ293866, SJ292868, SJ291867. From ON *hólmr* (island, useable part of a marshy area)

**CARR BRIDGE MEADOW, CARR FIELD HEY**

SJ289870, SJ291869. From ON *kjarr* (marsh)

**HIGHER & LOWER FLATS**

SJ295873. From ON *flatr* (flat)

### PENSBY AREA

**BRECK PLACE, BRECK HEY**

SJ301911, SJ302912. From ON *brekka* (hill, slope)

**PENSBY WOOD**

SJ266838. From ON *býr* (settlement)

**INTAKE**

SJ263833 *Inntak* "Enclosure" from ON *inntak*

**GILLS MEADOW, GILLS FIELD**

SJ71833, SJ272833. From ON *gil* (ravine/ hollow). Near the

bank of the Fender – see also entry for Gills Lane in Barnston area

## CARR HOUSE CROFT

SJ271841. From ON *kjarr* (marsh)

## POULTON CUM SEACOMBE AREA

### SEACOMBE FERRY

SJ227908 from ON *ferja* (ferry). Not known whether the ferry dates back to the settlement period

## PRENTON AREA

### KIRK HAY

SJ297862 "Church enclosure" from ON *kirkja* (church)

### RAKE HAY

SJ306865 "Enclosure by a lane" from ON *rák* (lane)

### INTAKE

SJ311865 *Inntak* "Enclosure" from ON *inntak*

### STACK YARD

SJ301860 "Stack or pile yard/ Pillar yard" from ON *stakkr* (stack, pile or pillar)

### FIVE ACRE HOLME

SJ294863. From ON *akr* (field, acre), ON *hólmr* (marsh-island, useable part of a marshy area)

## BRIDGE HOLME, TOP HOLME, LOWER HOLME, THE HOLME, HIGHER HOLME

SJ294865, SJ298864, SJ297865, SJ296866, SJ296864. From ON *hólmr* (marsh-island, useable part of a marshy area)

## RABY AREA

### RABY MERE, RABY MOUND, RABY VALE

SJ335809, SJ327789, SJ318808. From ON *rá* (boundary) ON *býr* (settlement).

### HABY TOWN

SJ310798. *Há-býr* "High-settlement" from ON *hár* (high) and ON *býr*. Haby Town is entered in the 1846 Tithe apportionment for Raby, but is probably a transcription error for Raby Town. There is a Haby also in Barnston

### FLATT HEY

SJ314796 "Flat enclosure" from ON *flatr* (flat)

### KIRKETT HEY

SJ307795 *Kirkja-gata* "The enclosure by the church/ church street" from ON *kirkja* (church), ON *gata* (street)

### RAKE HEY

SJ313804 "Enclosure by the lane" from ON *rák* (lane)

### SLACK HEY

SJ311795 "Enclosure by a hollow" from ON *slakki* (hollow)

### SLACKEY FIELD

SJ337806 "Field in the hollow" from ON *slakki* (hollow)

**PELLERDALE**
SJ338796 to SJ336791 *Píll-dalr* "Willow valley" from ON *píll* (willow), ON *dalr* (valley). Connects with Piladall (Hargrave/Blakeley part of Little Neston parish) and Piledale (Willaston area) – see Chapters 7, 10.

## SAUGHALL MASSIE AREA

**CARR FARM, CARR HOUSES, CARR MEADOW, NEW CARR, CARR, CARR HAY, OLD CARR MEADOW**
SJ242893, SJ247906, SJ239901, SJ235897, SJ239902, SJ241899, SJ242902. From ON *kjarr* (marsh)

**OLD CARR**
SJ245902 and SJ242900 "Old Marsh" from ON *kjarr* (marsh)

**CARR LANE**
SJ244902 to SJ249894 "Marsh lane" from ON *kjarr*

**LONG RAKE LANE (NOW HERON ROAD)**
SJ230900 to SJ245883 "Long Lane" from ON *rák* (lane)

**UFILYS BROW**
SJ245887 "Úfaldi's brow" from ON pers.n. *Úfaldi*

**WIMBRICKS**
SJ249882 *Hvin-brekka* "Gorsey slope on a hill" or "Gorse bank" from ON *hvin* (gorse), ON *brekka* (hill/ slope)- extends to Greasby

## SEACOMBE AREA: SEE POULTON CUM SEACOMBE AREA

## STORETON AREA

### GREAT STORETON, LITTLE STORETON
SJ305844, SJ304847 *Stór-tún* "Great farmstead" from ON *stór* (great), ON *tún* (farmstead)

### STORETON HILL
SJ314850 to SJ315840. From ON *stór*, ON *tún*

### RAKE LANE
SJ302889 to SJ305842. From ON *rák* (lane)

### RAKE HEY, RAKE DITCH
SJ303838, SJ303841. From ON *rák* (lane)

### RANSEL (RAUNCELRAKE AT 1323)
SJ291837 "Hut by rowan tree lane" from ON *raun, reynir* (rowan tree), ON *rák* (lane)

### LE GREMOTEHALLAND (1330)
SJ305844* *Griða-mót* "Place of a meeting under a truce" from ON *grið* (truce), ON *mót* (meeting)

### FLAT, FLATTBUTTS, UPPER FLAT, LOWER FLAT, HILL FLAT, SOUR FLATS
SJ309840, SJ305842, SJ302845, SJ300845, SJ313838, SJ311834. From ON *flatr* (flat). M53 motorway now cuts straight through Sour Flats

### INTACK
SJ306850 "Enclosure" from ON *inntak*

## THINGWALL AREA

### *THINGWELL (Field name), THINGWALL BROOK*
SJ282847, SJ285846 to SJ289846. *Þing-völlr*, from ON *þing* (Assembly), ON *völlr* (field). The site in Thingwall where the þing met was Cross Hill.

### *CROSS HILL*
SJ281844 from ON *kross* (cross). Site of the *þing* (Assembly)

### *SHOCKING DALE, DALE SHOOT, DALE HAY, DALE HEAPS*
SJ285842, SJ282843, SJ283842, SJ286843. From ON *dalr* (valley)

### *DALE END BROOK*
SJ280842 to SJ285841. From ON *dalr* (valley)

### *INTAKE*
SJ279842 *Inntak* "Enclosure" from ON *inntak*

## THORNTON HOUGH AREA

### *INTACK*
SJ315811 *Inntak* "Enclosure" from ON *inntak*

### *RAKE HEY*
SJ298805 "Enclosure by a lane" from ON *rák* (lane)

### *HESKETH GRANGE*
SJ302812 *Hesta-skeið* "Horse race track" from ON *hestur* (horse), ON *skeið* (track) – see also entry under Irby and Chapter 14

## THURSTASTON AREA

### THURSTASTON HILL, THURSTASTON COMMON
SJ245854, SJ245850. From ON pers.n. *Þorsteinn* (Thorsteinn)

### THOR'S STONE, THOR'S HILL
SJ244849, SJ245845. From ON *Þórr* (Thór).Antiquity uncertain

### STROMBY HAY
SJ241829 *Straumr-býr* "Settlement by a stream" from ON *straumr* (stream, current), *býr* (settlement)

### MECKANSEDGE
SJ253849. From ON *mikill* (great, large). Connects with Mickansedge in Irby parish

### STEYNCOLESDALE (1298, LATER TINKERS DALE)
SJ240829 to SJ241831 *Steinkell-dalr* from ON pers.n. *Steinkell*, ON *dalr* (valley)

### CROOK CORNER
SJ243833. From ON *krókr* (crook)

## TRANMERE AREA

### HINDERTON
SJ324880 *Hindri-tún* "Rear farmstead" or "Back of the farmstead" from ON *hindri* (back, rear), ON *tún* (farmstead)

### HINDERTON LANE
SJ320881 to SJ325877. From ON *hindri* (back, rear), ON *tún* (farmstead)

### ASKER DALE
SJ327877 *Askr-dalr* "Ash-tree valley" from ON *askr* (ash), ON *dalr* (valley)

### INTAKE
SJ316877 *Inntak* "Enclosure" from ON *inntak*

### SLACK FIELD
SJ331868 "Field at the hollow" from ON *slakki* (a hollow)

### KIRKS SLACKS
SJ320865 *Kirkja-slakki* "Hollow near the church" from ON *kirkja* (church), *slakki* (hollow)

### KIRKET HAY
SJ324860 "The enclosure by the church" from ON *kirkja*

### RAKE HAY
SJ318871 "Enclosure by the lane" from ON *rák*

### FAR STORETON FIELD, NEAR STORETON FIELD
SJ315859, SJ316861. From ON *stór* (great), ON *tún* (farmstead)

### RAYNILDES POOL (1323)
SJ330882 to SJ322885 "Ragnhildr's Pool" from ON pers.n. *Ragnhildr.*
Ragnhildr's Pool was lost in the construction of the docks, with the drained stream above it now the site of Dingle Road and the Valley Lodge in Devonshire Park

### GUNNEL POOL (1800)
SJ330872 "Gunnhildr's Pool" from ON pers.n. *Gunnhildr.*
Gunnhildr's Pool, recorded in 1529 as Gonnille Pool, represents another creak in from the Mersey now lost.

## UPTON AREA – SEE OVERCHURCH,

## WALLASEY AREA

### THE BRECK
SJ297917 "The hill/ slope" from ON *brekka*. See Chapter 14

### BRECK HAY
SJ296919. From ON *brekka* (hill/ slope)

### FIELD UNDER BRECK
SJ300912. From ON *brekka* (hill/ slope)

### THE CLYNSSE (1642)
SJ305908 "The Projecting rock" from ON *klint* (projecting rock). Large rock outcrop at the Breck.
**and/or at** SJ298942: Sandstone rock at Red Noses. See Chapter 14

### STONE BARK
SJ298934 "Stony cliff" from ON *bjarg* (cliff). See also entry for Liscard area

### STONY RAKE
SJ299920 "Stony lane" from ON *rák* (lane)

### LE SCHEPERAKE (1281)
SJ297920 "The sheep lane" from ON *rák* (lane). This lane was probably near Stony Rake: the "Liscard" rakes are too far away. See also Chapter 17.

### LE RAKE MILNE
SJ300920* "Mill by the lane" or "Lane by the mill" from ON *rák* (lane). See also Chapter 17

## *KIRKWAY (NOW CHURCH HILL)*
SJ269922. From ON *kirkja* (church)

## *WALLACRE ROAD (PROBABLY FORMERLY WALEY-CARR)*
SJ294917 to SJ297919. From ON *kjarr* (marsh) or ON *akr* (field, acre)

## *FEARNEY FLAT*
SJ300921. From ON *flatr* (flat)

## *INTAKE*
SJ299919 *Inntak* "Enclosure" from ON *inntak*

## *WYNNY HEY*
SJ299931 "Gorsey enclosure" from ON *hvin* (gorse)

## *KETTLE WELL GARDEN*
SJ293921 "Ketill's garden" from ON pers.n. *Ketill*

## *TOKESFORD (1397)*
SJ309909 "Tóki's ford" from ON pers.n. *Tóki*. Old crossing point on Wallasey pool

## *SEURYDZIS ALFLAND (1281)*
SJ295925* "Sigríðr's half-land" from ON pers.n. *Sigríðr*. See Chapter 17.

## *LE CROCISHIND (1280)*
SJ295920* "The crooked selions" from ON *krókr* (crook)

## WEST KIRBY AREA

### THE RUGS
SJ219858 "The Ridge" from ON *hryggr* (ridge)

### SLACK
SJ216865 "Hollow" from ON *slakki* (a hollow)

### KIRBYMOUNT
SJ223859. From ON *kirkja* (church), ON *býr* (settlement)

### ST. BRIDGET'S
SJ218864. From OIr pers.n. *Bridget, Brigid* – see also Chapter 13

### LINGDALE (ROAD)
SJ210872 to SJ213873 *Lyng-dalr* "Heather-dale" from ON *lyng* (heather), ON *dalr* (valley)

### THORSWAY
SJ226855 to SJ227857 from ON *Þórr* (Thór). Antiquity uncertain

### MICKELL BROOK (MICKENBROOK)
SJ217877* "Large brook" from ON *mikill* (great, large)

## WOODCHURCH AREA

### STACK YARD
SJ277867 "Stack or pile yard/Pillar yard" from ON *stakkr* (stack, pile, pillar)

### LOWER ACKERS, HIGHER ACKERS
SJ282866, SJ283866. From ON *akr* (field, acre) or *kjarr* (marsh)

# Chapter 7
## MINOR VIKING PLACE NAMES OUTSIDE THE WIRRAL-NORSE ENCLAVE

As with Chapter 6, for the enthusiast who wants to find/ visit these places a 1:50000 scale Landranger Ordnance Survey map is sufficient, although the 1:25000 and 1:10000 maps are better! Again, where there is uncertainty about the precise location, an asterisk * is placed against the Ordnance Survey coordinates.

### BROMBOROUGH AREA

#### *BROMBOROUGH COURT HOUSE*
SJ345842. Large ditched site (Court House no longer exists) along with Red or "Bloody" Hill in Storeton (Chapter 6) and possibly Wargraves at SJ357813 believed to have been a key site in the battle of Brunanburh (937AD) – see Chapter 11

#### *LATHEGESTFELD (1412)*
SJ357828*. J. Dodgson[10] suggests "Unwelcome guests field" from ON *leiðr* or OE *lað* (unwelcome) and ON *gestr* or OE *gest* ('a stranger, a traveller, a visitor'). He says also "Professor Sørensen suggests that Lathegest may represent an ON pers.n. *Leiðgestr*, ('the unwelcome visitor'), analagous with the similar ON pers.n. *Leiðulfr* – ('the unwelcome wolf')." These interpretations may refer to some local conflict in the area. More recent opinion however[11] suggests the first ON element is *leiða* "to lead", so *Leiðgestr* means "visiting guide's" or "visitor's guide".

---

[10] Place Names of Cheshire Part IV, page 244.
[11] Suggested by Magnus Magnusson. Professor Jan Ragnar Hagland agrees and has indicated this would also fit in with the few other names on *Leið*- that are recorded.

81

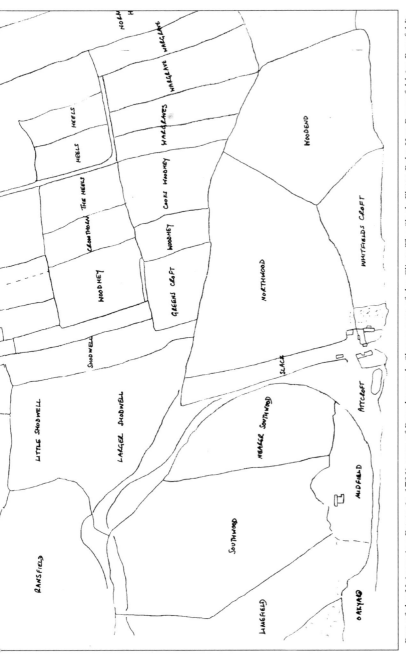

Part of the Mainwaring Estate (c. 1731) map of Bromborough. Shows part of the Clints, The Slack, Flatts, Rake Hey, Rawnsfield (as Ransfeld) and the Wargraves. By the time of the 1841 Tithe Map, Rawnsfeld and The Slack had gone and were part of an area marked "Park" and "Plantation" respectively. Courtesy of Mrs Susan Nicholson, Bromborough Society

**THE RAKE**
SJ345819 to SJ347821 "The lane" from ON *rák* (lane)

**MARK RAKE**
SJ346822 to SJ350824 "Mark lane" from ON *rák* (lane)

**RAKEHOUSE, RAKE HEY, RAKE CROFT, ELLIS' LOWER RAKE HEY**
SJ348845, SJ346821, SJ342819, SJ341824. From ON *rák* (lane)

**THE SLACK (1731)**
SJ360821 "Hollow" from ON *slakki* (a hollow). At the top end of what is now Eastham Country Park. Recorded on the 1731 Mainwaring estate map, but not on the 1834 Tithe map.

**ACRE SLACK/ ACRE SLACK WOOD**
SJ339815 "Acre hollow" from ON *akr* (field, acre), ON *slakki* (a hollow). Not connected to "The Slack" but on the western side of Bromborough, across the railway line., south of Bromborough Rake railway station

**THE CLINTS**
SJ345827 "The projecting rocks" from ON *klintir* (projecting rocks) – see Chapter 14.

**WOOD CLINTS**
SJ345826 "Wood at/near the projecting rocks" from ON *klintir* (projecting rocks) – see Chapter 14

**INTAKE**
SJ344820 *Inntak* "Enclosure" from ON *inntak*

**BROCKS DALE**
SJ342820 "Brocks valley" from ON *dalr* (valley)

**FLATTS**

SJ346826. From ON *flatr* (flat)

**RAWNESFELD (1440)**

SJ358817 "Ragnald's field" from ON pers.n. *Ragnaldr* or "Raven's field" from ON *hrafn* (raven). See also entry for "Rawnuesfeld" in Whitby area

**LE SKEREYORDE (1412)**

SJ352847 "Fish trap at the skerry" from ON *sker* (skerry)

## BURTON POINT AREA

**FIDDLESTONE, FIDDLESTON PLANTATION, FIDDLESTON HAY**

SJ326750, SJ327749, SJ326751. From ON pers.n. *Fiðill*, and possibly ON *tún* (farmstead)

**THE CHURCH RAKE, RAKE HEY**

SJ317742, SJ320736. From ON *rák* (lane)

**RAKE CROFT**

SJ322748, SJ316743. From ON *rák* (lane)

**SLACK LAKE (& FIELD)**

SJ311748 "Lake (& field) at a hollow". From ON *slakki* (a hollow)

**DENHALL FIELD, DENHALL HAY**

SJ320747, SJ303749. From ON *Danir* (Danes) – see entry for Ness area

**MOORE FLAT**

SJ320738. From ON *flatr* (flat)

## CROOKED FLAT
SJ329748. From ON *krókr* (crook), ON *flatr* (flat)

### CAPENHURST AREA

## INTAKE
SJ376732 *Inntak* "Enclosure" from ON *inntak*

## INGRIESSICHE (1340)
SJ370735* "Ingrid's stream" from ON pers.n. *Ingríðr*

### CHILDER THORNTON AREA
(See also page 4 of *Wirral and its Viking Heritage*)

## LOWFIELDS & HOUSE
SJ348779. From ON *lágr* (low). Links with Loghfeld in Little Sutton parish

## CROOK CROFT (1704)
SJ366780. From ON *krókr* (crook). Links with Croketcroft in Eastham

## RAKE OR GOOSE PASTURE, RAKE CROFT, RAKE PART, OLD RAKE
SJ349771, SJ363772, SJ362775, SJ360770*. From ON *rák* (lane)

## RAKE LANE (1831)
SJ359772 to SJ365774. From ON *rák* (lane)

### CHORLTON AREA

## ROSS CROFT
SJ306732. From ON *rauðr* (red)

## EASTHAM AREA

### EASTHAM RAKE
SJ347793 "Eastham lane" from ON *rák* (lane). See also entry under Willaston area

### RAKE INCLOSURE
SJ353796, SJ355798 "Enclosure by a lane" from ON *rák* (lane)

### RAKE HEY
SJ351797 "Enclosure by a lane" from ON *rák* (lane)

### BRIDGETS (LOWER & HIGHER), NEARER BRIDGETS, BIG BRIDGETS
SJ363788, SJ363789, SJ361788 from OIr pers.n. *Bridget, Brigid* – joint patron saint of Ireland – see Chapter 13

### LOWER FLATS
SJ364787. From ON *flatr* (flat)

### CROKETCROFT (1440)
SJ366787 "Crooked croft" from ON *krókr*. Links with Crook Croft in Childer Thornton

## ELLESMERE PORT AREA – SEE WHITBY AREA

## GREAT MOLLINGTON AREA

### TORRALD FYELD (NOW TOWNFIELD LANE)
SJ378708 to SJ365703 "Thorald's field" from ON pers.n. *Þóraldr*

## GREAT SAUGHALL AREA

### DALES
SJ365694 from ON *dalr* (valley)

### STACK YARD
SJ371703 "Stack or pile yard/ Pillar Yard" from ON *stakkr* (stack, pile or pillar)

### SLACK CROFT
SJ362706, SJ360702 "Croft at a hollow" from ON *slakki* (a hollow)

### SYLLABY BUTT, SYLLABY CROFT & FIELD
SJ364695, SJ363693 *Sylla-býr* "Sylla's settlement" from ON pers.n. *Sylla*(?), ON *býr* (settlement)

### BARK CORNER
SJ365728 from ON *bjarg* (cliff)

### BARK GATE
SJ362706 from ON *bjarg* (cliff), ON *gata* (street)

### WHITBY'S ACRE (WHITBYTYLTH, 1440)
SJ368708 "Cultivated land belonging to Whitby" from ON *hviti* (white), ON *býr* (settlement)

## GREAT STANNEY AREA

### HOLMLAKE
SJ419754 "Lake by the marsh-island" from ON *hólmr* (marsh island, or useable area in a marsh). Links with Holmlache in Stanlow

## RAKEMORE FIELD (1600)
SJ405750* "Field by a lane" from ON *rák* (lane)

## HIGHER BEBINGTON AREA

### RAKE HAY
SJ326853 "Enclosure by a lane" from ON *rák* (lane)

### STORETON HILL
SJ314850 to SJ315840. From ON *stór* (great), ON *tún* (farmstead). See also Storeton area. Likely boundary with main Norse enclave

### LE SCHAMFORLONG (1300)
SJ319848* "The short furlong" from ON *skammr* (short)

### ROCK FERRY
SJ330864. From ON *ferja* (ferry). Not known if it goes back to the settlement period

## HOOTON AREA

### STACK WOOD (NOW CHURCH WOOD)
SJ373778 "Stack or pile wood/ Pillar wood" from ON *stakkr* (stack, pile or pillar)

### LE SKER EN HOOTON (NOW POOLE HALL ROCKS)
SJ389791 "The skerry at or near Hooton" from ON *sker* (skerry)

### KETILSPOL (1402)
SJ379779 "Ketill's Creek" from ON pers.n. *Ketill*. Site of what is now Riveacre park.

## LEDSHAM AREA

### BADGERSRAKE (COVERT)
SJ343752 "Badger's lane" from ON *rák* (lane). See also entries under Puddington and Willaston areas

### CROOK LOONS
SJ361744 "Crooked selions" from ON *krókr* (crook)

### FLAT HEY, LITTLE FLAT HEY, BIG FLAT HEY, COOPERS FLAT
SJ362747, SJ368743, SJ366743, SJ351751. From ON *flatr* (flat)

### INNTAK
SJ363750, SJ356740 *Inntak* "Enclosure" from ON *inntak*

### INTACK & LONG CROFT
SJ352778 *Inntak* "Enclosure" from ON *inntak*

## LITTLE SAUGHALL AREA

### KIRKLAND HO, KIRKS FIELD
SJ370690*, SJ311692. From ON *kirkja* (church)

## LITTLE STANNEY AREA

### RAKE HALL
SJ412741. From ON *rák* (lane)

## LITTLE SUTTON AREA

### LOGHFELD (1432)
SJ348774 "Low-field" from ON *lágr* (low). Links with Lowfields in Childer Thornton parish

### OLD RAKE, RAKE CROFT, RAKE
SJ361769, SJ370769, SJ365769. From ON *rák* (lane)

### RAKE LANE (1831)
SJ359772 to SJ365774. From ON *rák* (lane)

### LE CLYNTES (1440)
SJ371776. From ON *klintir* (projecting rocks). Appears to be none in the parish which fits the bill. However, *klintir* is also taken to mean "tough large stones": there are some at the golf course.

## LOWER BEBINGTON AREA

### NEW FERRY
SJ344853. From ON *ferja* (ferry). Not known if it goes back to the settlement period

### KIRKET LANE (CHURCH ROAD)
SJ328841 to SJ333840 "The church lane" from ON *kirkja* (church)

### INTAKE
SJ327852 *Inntak* "Enclosure" from ON *inntak*

### HELLELOND (1300: NOW ELLENS LANE)
SJ335841 "Land at or near a hole or cave" from ON *hella/hellir* (hole/cave), ON *lundr* (grove). The same element *hella/ hellir,*

along with ON *býr* gives its name to the Norse outlier Helsby at SJ487757

## LE RAKE (1357)
SJ332841*. From ON rák (lane)

## NESS AREA

### DENHALL, DENNAH HEY, DENNAH MEADOW
SJ300748, SJ304752, SJ298753 "Danes spring" from ON *Danir* (Danes, of the Danes), OE *wælla* (spring)

### MICKWELL, MICKWELL BROW, MICKWELL COVERT
SJ303754, SJ305755, SJ303755. "Great spring" from ON *mikill* (great, large) and OE *wælla* (spring)

### GREAT & LITTLE DALE
SJ304753 "Great & Little valley". From ON *dalr* (valley)

### PIT DALE (1831)
SJ306758. From ON *dalr* (valley)

### STACK YARD
SJ303759 "Stack or pile yard/ Pillar yard" from ON *stakkr* (stack, pile or pillar)

### HATE FLAT
SJ304756. From ON *flatr* (flat)

## NETHERPOOL AREA – SEE WHITBY AREA

## OVERPOOL AREA – SEE WHITBY AREA

## POULTON CUM SPITAL AREA

### *LA STOPELRAKE (1406)*

SJ332812 "Lane or path to the stepping stones" from ON *rák* (lane). Stepping stones are in the stream at Raby Mill/Mere at the Poulton boundary

Stepping stones at Raby Mill at the border/boundary with Poulton - see *La Stopelrake* (Poulton-cum-Spital area). Photograph taken in period 1900-1905. Courtesy of Gavin Hunter

## PUDDINGTON AREA

### BADGER RAKE
SJ338754 "Badger lane" from ON *rák* (lane) see also entries under Ledsham and Willaston

### HIGHER RAKESIDE, LOWER RAKESIDE, GREEN RAKE, GREAT GREEN RAKE, LITTLE GREEN RAKE
SJ334734, SJ333734, SJ344737, SJ345737, SJ345736. From ON *rák* (lane)

### FLATS
SJ335738. From ON *flatr* (flat)

## STANLOW AREA

### HOLMLACHE (1209)
SJ421756 "Lake by the marsh-island" from ON *hólmr*. Links with Holmlake in Great Stanney

### INTACK (1554)
SJ432755* *Inntak* "Enclosure" from ON *inntak*

## WHITBY AREA

### BYMANS SLACKS
SJ412761* "Byman's hollow" from ON *slakki* (a hollow)

### CROOKLANDS, CROOKLOONS
SJ403765 "Crooked selions" from ON *krókr* (crook)

### INTAKE
SJ388782, SJ391775 *Inntak* "Enclosure" from ON *inntak*

### NEAR INTAKE, FAR INTAKE
SJ394755, SJ394754 from ON *inntak* (enclosure)

### BADGERSRAKE LANE
SJ398761 to SJ352763 "Badger lane" from ON *rák* (lane)

### RAKE MEADOW
SJ404768. From ON *rák* (lane)

### RAWNUESFELD (1440)
SJ406760* "Ragnaldr's field" from ON pers.n. *Ragnaldr*, or "Ravens Field" from ON *hrafn*. See also entry for Rawnsfeld in Bromborough area

### FLAT, HALWOODS FLAT
*SJ398761, SJ401761. From ON* flatr (flat)

## WILLASTON AREA

### BADGER'S RAKE
SJ338753 "Badger's lane" from ON *rák* (lane). See also entries under Ledsham area and Puddington area

### EASTHAM RAKE
SJ343785 to SJ358800. From ON *rák* (lane). See also entry under Eastham area

### RAKE END FIELD, RAKE END CROFT, NEW RAKE HEY, RAKE END MEADOW
SJ338779, SJ341778, SJ340780, SJ341781. From ON *rák* (lane)

### RAKE END & HEY
SJ344755. From ON *rák* (lane)

## INTAKE
SJ332776, SJ331781 *Inntak* "Enclosure" from ON *inntak*

## LITTLE INTAKE, TOP INTAKE
SJ329770, SJ331779. *Inntak* "Enclosure" from ON *inntak*

## STACK YARD
SJ328775 "Stack or pile yard/ Pillar yard" from ON *stakkr* (stack, pile or pillar)

## NESS ACRE, BIG NESS ACRE, NESS ACRE CROFT
SJ325775, SJ325772, SJ328771, From ON *akr* (field, acre)

## LEICHERICHEWALLEDALE (1309)
SJ346795 to SJ355777. From ON *dalr* (valley) – see Chapters 8 & 10

## MICKELDALE (1309)
SJ340818 to SJ342789 *Mikill-dalr* "Great valley" from ON *mikill* (great, large), ON *dalr* (valley). See also Blakeley/Hargrave part of Little Neston (Chap. 6). See also Chapters 8 & 10

## PILEDALE (1309)
SJ336791 to SJ332788 *Píll-dalr* "Willow valley" from ON *píll* (willow), ON *dalr* (valley). Connects with Pellerdale (Raby Parish, Chap. 6) and Piladall (Blakeley/Hargrave part of Little Neston (Chap. 6) . See also Chapters 8 & 10

## WOODBANK AREA

## SLACK CROFT
SJ342721. From ON *slakki* (a hollow)

### GRYMISGREUE (1463)

SJ344722* "*Grímr's* wood" or "*Óðinn's* wood". From ON pers.n. *Grímr*: the same name appears in a list of pre-Domesday landowners from the Wirral (see Chapter 17). *Grímr* was also a personal name or by-name of *Óðinn*, the god.

### LE STORRGREVES

SJ344718* "The great woods" from ON *stór* (great, large)

# Chapter 8
## SOME INTERESTING EXTRACTS FROM THE CHESHIRE SHEAF AND JOHN RYLANDS CHARTERS

Besides J. McNeal Dodgson's four part treatise on Cheshire Place Names and the Tithe Maps and Apportionments at the Chester Record Office, further useful sources in helping to pinpoint the meaning and locations of some of the places have been the *Cheshire Sheaf* and also the ancient Charters of the Wirral now stored at the John Rylands Library at the University of Manchester. The *Cheshire Sheaf* was a monthly journal started in the late 19th century and provided until recently a useful forum for historical and other discussion about the Wirral. Other articles from the *Sheaf* will be quoted in subsequent chapters but we include here five topics of definite Wirral Norse interest. One concerns *The Arno* in Oxton, another concerns some lost *Thwaites* in Bidston, the final three deal with a series of field names in Grange, Caldy (including the *Kneckyn* - the old name for Caldy Hill), and the West Kirby/Newton Area, the latter of which includes some interesting detective work presumbly undertaken by William Fergusson Irvine, a very prominent local historian at the turn of the 19th century.

### 1. Arno Hill in Oxton
This hill or mound, just off Storeton Road and shown in Chapter 6 is named after the Old Norse personal name *Árni* and the 1909 writer (A.H.Arkle of Oxton) is speculating on its relation with a similar place near Whitby in Yorkshire. It is still unclear as to whether *Árni* is buried here.

FROM CHESHIRE SHEAF, VOL. 7, DECEMBER 1909, PAGES 101-102, EXTRACT FROM ARTICLE 1437

I have seen no reply to my enquiry respecting the reason for this name which is applied to the small hill at the south end of the Oxton ridge. I therefore venture a suggestion which has occurred to me through reading a paragraph in Young's "History of Whitby". It seems that there is an "Arno Cross" on the North Yorkshire Moors near Rosedale, and the author referred to suggests that this is a corruption of Arne Houe or Howe as it stands on a Howe, Arne being a family name. Now it may appear at first sight that there is no connection with the "Arno" in Oxton, but on looking further into the matter and trying to imagine how the place looked before it was quarried and before any houses had been built, one cannot be struck by the fact that the hill must have presented an appearance exactly corresponding to that of a Howe or pointed little Hill. From this point there is now a very beautiful and extensive view, but in old times the view must have taken a still wider area of many miles in extent and therefore is just the place for the burial of some ancient Chieftain.... *Oxton. A.H.Arkle.*

## 2. Utterthwaite and Inderthwaite in Bidston

This 1902 article by William Fergusson Irvine, who quotes part of the rental of the Earl of Derby identifies two former *þveits* now lost: Uttertwaite (ON: *úttar* or *utar* "outer" and *þveit* "clearing") and Indertwaite (ON: *innar* "inner")

FROM CHESHIRE SHEAF, VOL. 4, MARCH 1902, PAGE 23-25. EXTRACT FROM ARTICLE 589: RENTAL OF THE (2ND) EARL OF DERBY'S PROPERTY IN WIRRAL, 1521-2

Uttertwaite and Indertwaite or as we should now call them Outer Thwaite and Inner Thwaite, are probably represented by the modern Tassey's Thwaite, Whinney Thwaite, Spencer's Thwaite and the rest of the group of fields known as the Thwaites down on the Bidston Moss... *Wm. Fergusson Irvine*

*The rental:* "Hankyn Hycoke and another for one close called Uttertwaite containing 40 acres of land, 40s 0d; Richard Smyth for a close of land called Indertwaite containing 24 acres of land, 24s 0d"

### 3. Some Norse Field Names in Grange

This 1960 article concerns some rakes (ON *rák*), some holms (ON *hólmr*), Scamblants (ON *skammr*), Mecca Brook (ON *mjúkr*) and Carr Hey (ON *kjarr*) in Grange. The article is based on the 1777 marriage of one of the Glegge family (who give their name to the Glegg Arms public house in Gayton). The writer poses the question about the continued existence of some of these rakes, places and stream (Mecca Brook):

FROM CHESHIRE SHEAF, VOL. 55, MARCH, 1960, PAGE 30. EXTRACT FROM ARTICLE 10579

In the Hayes-Lyon collection at Chester Castle there is an extract from the Marriage Settlement of Mrs Sidney Glegge, 22nd Jan. 1777, which is interesting for the number of field names given in Grange *alias* Caldey Grange: They are: Little Rake Hey, Scamblants, Mecca Brook, Nearer South Holme, Further South Holme, Holme's Yard, North Holm, Further Rake Hey, Rake Hey, Rake Hey Meadow, Middle Rake Hey, Carr Hey, all belonging to William Glegge and in several tenancies. It would be interesting to know whether any of these names survive and how many of these fields still exist

### 4. Some Norse Field Names in Caldy

This trio of 1903 articles, again written by William Fergusson Irvine, records some old rental documents of 1453-4 highlighting the Kneckyn (OIr *cnocc*), The Rake (ON *rák*), Kyrke Cross (ON *kirkja, kross*), Ascow (ON *askr, skógr*), Soutery Londe (ON *sútari*), Brankers Pitt (ON *brenna*), Wranglandes (ON *vrangr* or *rangr*) and The Wro (ON *vrá* or *rá*) in Little Caldy. All these place names had been lost by the time the 19ᵗʰ Century tithe maps and apportionments were compiled. According to J. Dodgson the "*kirkja*" or church to which The Kyrke Cross refers is probably St. Bridgets at West Kirby.

FROM CHESHIRE SHEAF, VOL. 5, APRIL 1903, PAGE 35-37. EXTRACT FROM ARTICLE 825: THE MANOR OF LITTLE CALDY IN WIRRAL IN 1453-4

The following extracts are from the Rental of Thomas Norris of Speke, co. Lancaster, dated 1453-4. The original, which includes an account of his Lancashire property, is on a roll of vellum 13 feet 4 inches long and 7 inches wide, and is now among the Aston Hall muniments. It is written closely on both sides in black ink with capitals and paragraphs picked out in red. There are notes and additions made about the year 1545, in a later hand, apparently by Sir William Norris, Kt., great-grandson of Thomas Norris, to whom the property had descended.

One of the most interesting features of this Rental is the way in which the different holdings are described shewing the common field system of cultivation of active working. In each farm (as we shall now call it) the arable is split up into many small strips or "hallands" lying in different open fields... The portion relating to Little Caldy in Wirral shows that there were only three landowners in the manor. Thomas Norris himself, William Whitmore and Hugh Egerton ... I would suggest that the words "one land" mean a quarter of an acre, "one halland" one half-land or one-eighth of an acre, and "one ferthing" one sixteenth. It must be borne in mind that an acre in the open field system was not a square figure, but an oblong, the normal length of which was a "furrowlong" or furlong, i.e. 220 yards, and the normal width 22 yards... "A butt" was probably the same as a "ferthing".... The field names mentioned in this account of Caldy are extremely interesting, and many of them can be traced to the present day: ... KNEKYN is not easily identified but is evidently some rising land, possibly Caldy Field itself, as the different fields are spoken of as being "under" Knekyn. It is doubtless an interesting survival of a Celtic place name, being a form of the common Irish word knock, meaning a hill.... THE RAKE would be a lane leading out on the common or waste, and may be represented now by the road running westwards to the shore. The mention of KYRKE CROSSE is very interesting and must refer to some wayside cross, probably on the Caldy Road, leading to the Parish Church.

RENTAL DE CALDAY YN WERALL: ITEM. Oon hallandundyr Knekyn the on ende este, the other weste lyinge betwene the londe of William Whitmore on both sydes.... ITEM. Oon londe leynge in the SOUTERY LONDE schotande este and weste betwene the londe of Thomas Norres on ye sowthe syde & Egyrton on ye northe syde... ITEM. Alle the grounde callyt Ascow... lyynge betwis Calday Hay and Thomas Lytylle... ITEM. Two hallandes besyde the rake, W. Whitmore on the sowthe syde & THE RAKE on the northe syde.... ITEM. Oon hallande undyr the KYRKE CROSSE schotynge est & west, Egyrton on the northe syde & Whitmore on the sowthe syde.... ITEM. Oon odyr hallande under the KYRKE CROSSE schotynge est and west betwene the londe of W. Whitmore on ayther side.

FROM CHESHIRE SHEAF, VOL. 5, MAY 1903, PAGE 46-48
EXTRACT FROM ARTICLE 836: THE MANOR OF LITTLE CALDY IN WIRRAL IN 1453-4. II.

Key (for locations given in square brackets in this article and the following 2 articles): H.E.: Hugh Egyrton; W.W., and –W.: William Whitmore; T.N.: Thomas Norris. N. North; S. South; E. East; W. West. N.E. north east, S.W. south west etc.

(Of the holdings of Richard Andrew:) ...One halland on the

north side of The Rake [E. & W.]... Another halland on the south side of The Rake [E. & W. -W. on the S.]... One halland "be the sowthe cornelle of Calday Hey" [N.E. & S.W.-W on both sides]...One halland in the Wro [N.&S. -W.W. on both sides] ... One halland undyr Kneckyn [E.&W. - W.W. on either side] ... Two hallandes undyr Knekyn "schotynge a pon "The Brankers Pytte" [E. & W.]. (Of the holdings of Thomas Clerke:) ...Two buttes schottynge apon Knekyn [E. & W.] ... (E. & W.] ... All the grounde callyt Ascow leynge betwix Calday Hay & Thos. Lytyll.

FROM CHESHIRE SHEAF, VOL. 5, JUNE 1903, PAGE 54-55
EXTRACT FROM ARTICLE 836: THE MANOR OF LITTLE CALDY IN WIRRAL IN 1453-4. III.
From the second entry under Thomas Letyll's holding the position of The Rake will be gathered. Croft Melayne, now divided into Lower and Higher Croft Mellon lies to the north of the lane leading down from the Caldy Road to the old Wharf and Lime Kiln, therefore it is evident that this is the lane known as the Rake. ... *Wm. Fergusson Irvine*

(Of the holdings of Thomas Letyll). Thomas Letyll holds one messuage and Holleys one londe in Crofte Melayne [E. &W.. -W.W. on S.,T.N. on N.] ... One halland in the same [E. & W., -T.N. on N. & the Rake on the S.] ... One halland undyr the Kyrke Crosse [E.&W. -W.W. on N., H.E. on S.]. ... One hadlande in the Grede Buttes that the Wranglandes schotyn apon [E. & S.W.]. One hallande in the Wranglandes [N.W. & S.E. W.W. on both sides] ... One hadlonde that the Wrangolondes schotynge on [E. & W. - W.W. on N., H.E. on S.] ... One londe in the Sowterslonde [E. & W., - H.E. on S. & T.N. on N.]. One hallande undyr Kneckyn [E. & W. - W.W. on both sides]... One hallonde under the Kyrke Crosse [E. & W.]. One hallonde lyinge by the Rake [E. & W. - W.W. on one side & E on other] ... A hallonde on the Kneckyn [E. & W. - W.W.

on both sides]. Another hallonde under Kneckyn [E.&W. -W.W. on both sides]…One hallande at the Townys Ende callyt the Wro [N. & S. - W.W. on both]. One other hallande lying in the Wro [N. & S.] One hallonde under the Kneckyn [E. & W. -W.W. on both].

## 5. Some Norse Field Names in West Kirby and Newton

This 1906 article identifies Mackel brock or Mickenbrook (ON *mikill*) in West Kirby and the Newton Rakes and Breken (ON *rák, brekka*). Of particular interest is the Harleian manuscript on which this Cheshire Sheaf article is based – an incomplete section with reference to the *brekka* (slope/hill) at Newton is apparently missed in the printed version by the writer, later entered in handwritten form in the copy which now resides in the Chester Record Office.

FROM CHESHIRE SHEAF, VOL. 6, OCTOBER, 1906, PAGE 83-83. EXTRACT FROM ARTICLE 1143: THE RECTORY OF WEST KIRBY IN THE REIGN OF CHARLES I

The following transcript of a document copied from the Harleian MS. No. 2009 f.337 … in Great Caldey from a place called the Mackel brock to Newton rake.. all the Field called Stoken South [or Souch] Croft up to the heath of Dalbyrston… Hynderston Raw lymefeild fro Hemedale to Newton Rake … And in Newbold…all the field length from the Court of Newbold that goes to Holedale and so thaverton [therefrom] to the Smith's Shockes with the Middle Furlonges and soe from the Smith's Shockes all that shootes on the Court of Newboldout-taken 17 butts next the meadowe with the headloonds that shooten the ends to Henedale.

The Editor of the Sheaf adds the following footnotes: (1) Mackell Brock. Query Mickenbrook a field on the left of the road from Grange to Newton?. (2) Newton Rake; probably the road from Newton towards Little Caldy. (3) Stoken Souch. There was a field called Stokum Hey on the left between Grange and Newton.

The copy of Cheshire Sheaf in the Chester Record Office has the following handwritten comments in the margin. These comments, possibly the result of some "detective work" by Wm. Fergusson Irvine, whom we know donated a set of Cheshire Sheafs to the Record Office - expand on a section in the Harleian mss, left as just ...[incomplete] ... in the Sheaf: *The field of [blank] that the monkes and [blank] of Newton breken [blank] brock furlongs ..*

## John Rylands Charters

Ancient charters dating back almost to Domesday, have also been a very valuable source of place-name information: the earlier ones are all in Latin. In Chapter 17 we focus on a Charter from 1280 describing *Sigríðr* and her "Half-land". Here we show two others: John Rylands Charter (JRC) number 1438, dating from the year 1318 and identifying *Rauncelrake* (ON *raun* or *reynir, rák*) in Storeton Parish; the second is JRC 1604 from the year 1412 identifying *le Skereyorde* (ON *sker*) and *Lathegestfeld* (ON - *leið-gestr*) in Bromborough.

**John Rylands Charter number 1438**
**(dated 1318) :**
**Rauncelrake**

Let it be known to all people both present and future that we, William of Stanley and my wife Johanna, have given, granted and by this present our charter have confirmed to Adam our son, two messuages and four bovates of land... Furthermore we have given, granted and by this present our charter have confirmed to the same Adam our full share of the newly broken land which lies between the boundaries of Brimstage and the open field of Storeton beside Rauncele Rake; and further we have given, granted and by this present our charter have confirmed to the said Adam a plot of land called the Newefild ('the New Field') with appurtenances in the aforesaid vill of Storeton which we held from Richard of Benfield, lying along the breadth of the open field of Hu'bulston' (Umberstone) to the white site extending from the turbary road to Harriespole ('Henry's Pool')...

Translation of the relevant sections and comments (in brackets) by Paul Cavill

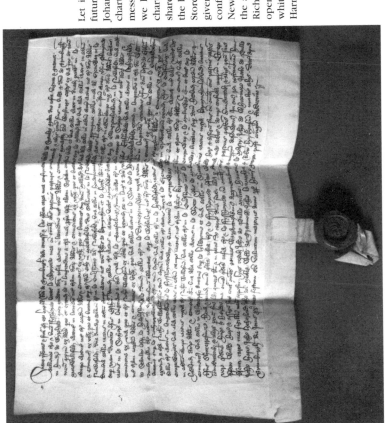

107

## John Rylands Charter number
## *1604* (dated 1412):
## le Skereyorde and Lathegestfeld

Let it be known to all people both present and future that I, Hugo son of Richard of Bromborough, have given, granted and by this present my charter have confirmed to William of Stanley, knight, two tofts (building sites) and 24 selions of land and one Fyssheyorde ('Fish-trap') called the Skereyorde ('fish-trap at the skerry')... [Of these selions] one selion lying in Lathegestfeld (? 'unwelcome visitor's field') ...

Translation of the relevant sections and comments (in brackets) by Paul Cavill

**Wirral-Norse activities**

Having now satisfied the "anorak" in identifying where to find all or at least most of the places of Norse interest, we can now examine in some detail the activities of these people, and in particular their relations to the English who themselves had come from Northern Europe and spoke a language not too dissimilar from their own. A Norseman could probably make himself understood to an Englishman and *vice-versa*. When they colonised, the Norse, together with their Irish followers would not have given new place names to ones already established by the English and probably would have adopted them as they were originally or just modified them slightly, as for example, in the case of *Greasby*. In some cases a cross-border pidgin word became adopted: the *rakes* are an outstanding example here, as we have already noted in Chapter 3 and considered in some detail in the *Wirral and its Viking Heritage* book. It is significant that many of the new names given by the Norsemen are for fairly unattractive areas - such as the *carr's* and *holm's*, areas with which the few people who were in the area before had just not bothered about. This adds further credance to the Ingimund story: the willingness of the English Queen Æthelflaed to release lands to an alien population – since the lands were hardly used anyway – followed by the subsequent restlessness of the Scandinavian masses and desire for better lands after the colony had been established.

# Chapter 9
## "VISITS" TO CHESTER

*"The Wirral colony began a programme of vigorous and occasionally armed expansion almost immediately after its establishment, towards the better lands of the English districts to the south"* John McNeal Dodgson, Cheshire Historian, 1928-1990

The large number of places not only inside the border of the main Norse enclave but also outside demonstrates that after being given permission by the Queen of the English to settle in the less fertile areas of north-west Wirral, the Wirral Norse were soon engaging in an active programme of expansion towards the rest of the Wirral and the surrounding hinterland – this included the coastal areas across the shores on the Wales side of the Dee (e.g. Talacre in Flint) and the Liverpool side of the Mersey (establishing places like Crosby and Formby). This programme of expansion also extended to Chester.

Ingimund's story – as related in Chapter 1 – tells of the Wirral Norse's repeated attempts to secure Chester by military means, working with their Danish and Irish allies: although success had not been achieved by the end of the story, it ends with the statement *"but it was not long after that before the Norsemen came to do battle again..."* Eventually they did achieve some success. Abandoning an aggressive approach and adopting a more subtle one instead seems to have paid dividends, with a community developing in the south of the city paralleled by an active involvement in the financial organisation of not only Wirral but also Chester: we know this for a number of reasons. One of the 10th century moneyers from the area bore clear Irish-Norse origins with the name of

*Irfara* (ON derivation "Ireland journeyer") and others included *Oslac* and *Mœldomen*. These were just three of a large number of moneyers bearing Norse names between 910 and 1066 in Chester, a proportion far higher than many mints elsewhere in England even during the period of Scandinavian rule by King Canute (1017–1035) and his sons Harald (until 1040) and Hardacanute (1042). By Canute's time an outlier Norse community from the main Wirral enclave appears to have been well established in the Handbridge area south of the city. The mark of these people on the financial, administrative and legal arrangements of Chester and its shire remained at least until the 13th century. One Norseman, *Gunnor*, held one third of the then important episcopal manor of Redcliff. The twelve iudices of the city, mentioned in 1086 as chosen from the men of the king, bishop, and earl, and obliged to attend the Chester hundred court, resembled the lawmen of the Scandinavian boroughs. A powerful Norse community at Handbridge was reflected in terms of its assessment by using the Scandinavian *carucates* as a measure and not the English *hides*.

As described by A. Thacker on p255 of Harris and Thacker's edited book *Victoria History of the County of Chester vol I*, the financial gurus of the Handbridge/South Chester Wirral-Norse outlier appeared to be much concerned with minting and trade links not only with English districts but also with the Norse controlled areas of Dublin, Isle of Man and York. Clear evidence of these links has come from significant archaeological finds, with several characteristic ring-headed pins discovered. Fragments of arm rings and brooches dated to 970-980AD discovered in Castle Esplanade in Chester resemble strongly jewellery discovered at Ballaquayle (Isle of Man). A Norse brooch discovered in Princess Street, Chester, is identical to one discovered in Dublin and was doubtless made from the same mould. Timberwork in cellared structures to the south of the Roman wall is of the same form as structures excavated in Dublin and the old Viking kingdom of York.

Although not as overwhelming as in the main Wirral enclave, place-name evidence is not absent from its South Chester outlier. *Clippe Gate* (near Bridge gate) and *Wolfeld's Gate* (the old name for Newgate), derive from the Norse personal names of the man *Klyppr* and woman *Úlfhildr* respectively and two churches – still present today – have Norse-Irish roots. One of these is St. Olave's lying just south of the city wall: this church was dedicated to the Norwegian king, Ólaf Haraldsson, "King Ólaf the Saint" (died 1030). Other churches dedicated to the same saint can be found in Bergen, Trondheim and London. The other church is St. Bridget's, which, like its West Kirby counterpart (Chapter 13) was dedicated to the Irish saint Bridget (OIr *Brigid*). St. Bridget – and the Christianity and possible remaining paganism of the Wirral Norsemen - will be considered in Chapter 13.

# Chapter 10
## THE SOUTH-EAST BORDER:
## RABY AND WILLOW VALLEY

The following is a further pair of extracts from the *Cheshire Sheaf*. These particular articles – based on a 1309 entry in the Chester Plea Roll - are interesting as they consider the border area between the Scandinavian enclave in the North and West of the Wirral and the more English districts to the South and East. They highlight the stream at Mickledale (from Old Norse *Mikill-dalr* "Great Valley"), which later became Plymyard Dale: the stream is part of Dibbinsdale Brook. This "Great Valley" once repesented the Eastern boundary between (Norse) Raby & the Hargrave area of Little Neston, and the "English" districts of Bromborough and Eastham to the east. The southern boundary is between Raby and Willaston, again initially demarked by Mickledale. These articles also highlight what must have been an old viking beauty spot, *Píll-dalr* which translates as "Willow Valley".

FROM CHESHIRE SHEAF, VOL. 24, DECEMBER, 1928, PAGES 88-89.
EXTRACT FROM ARTICLE 5753 (BOUNDS BETWEEN WILLASTON AND
LITTLE NESTON IN 1309)

In the Chester Plea Roll 22 (m.1d.) is recorded the following perambulation, made about 1309, concerning the bounds between the lands of Agnes, widow of Warin de Meynwarin in Wilaston and those of Thomas le Coroun, Lucy widow of Hugh le Coroun and Margaret widow of John le Coroun in Little Neston. "The bounds begin in the east at Mickledale, where a stone is placed called Richardston le Reve in the middle between Piledale and a place where the watercourse (ducta) of Lecherichewalledale falls into the watercourse of Mickeldale; and so from that stone in a line westward by marked stones as far as the mereston called Vilkynstane on this side of the Harestane as far as the the middle of Midlethrinlowe"

FROM CHESHIRE SHEAF, VOL. 25, JANUARY 9, 1929 PAGE 3. EXTRACT FROM ARTICLE 5762 (THE BOUNDS BETWEEN WILLASTON AND LITTLE NESTON IN 1309)

The boundaries in the 1309 deed begin at the stream running northwards through Mickledale now known as Plymyard Dale, a stream which eventually empties itself into Bromborough Pool. The first boundary stone bears the curious name "Richardston le Reve" and no doubt stood at the S.E. corner of the field now called Rye Hey; this point is about half way between where Piledale now called Pellerdale embouches on Mickledale, and where "Leicherichewalledale" joins Mickledale. The latter name appears to represent the little stream which now runs through the Sewage Works close to the main Chester (railway) line, and which joins Mickledale on the east bank. From this stone the boundary runs westward, the deed tells us, to another "Mereston" called "Vilkynstane" on this side of Harestane. Vilkynstane probably still exists and is represented by a slight bend in the hedge at the N.W. corner of Big Fox Holes at a distance of about three furlongs from Mickledale".

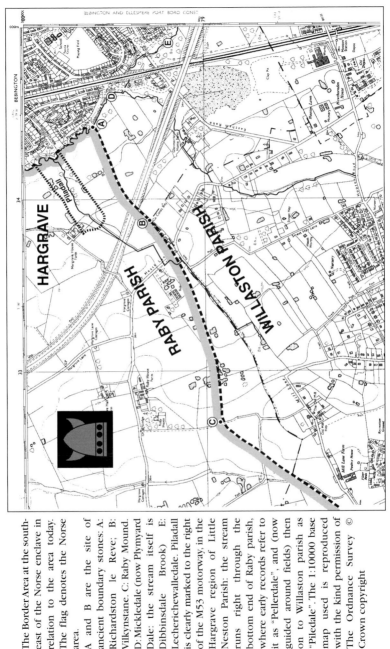

The Border Area at the south-east of the Norse enclave in relation to the area today. The flag denotes the Norse area.

A and B are the site of ancient boundary stones: A: Richardstone le Reve; B: Vilkynstane. C: Raby Mound. D: Mickledale (now Plymyard Dale: the stream itself is Dibbinsdale Brook) E: Lecherichewalledale. Piladall is clearly marked to the right of the M53 motorway, in the Hargrave region of Little Neston Parish: the stream runs right through the bottom end of Raby parish, where early records refer to it as "Pellerdale", and (now guided around fields) then on to Willaston parish as "Piledale". The 1:10000 base map used is reproduced with the kind permission of The Ordnance Survey © Crown copyright

The southern boundary continues along Mill Lane and then Damhead Lane onto Ness. At least three places in neighbouring parishes in the Wirral bear the name "Willow Valley", from *píll* (willow) and *dalr* (valley). These are Pellerdale recorded in Raby Parish, Piledale recorded in Willaston Parish, and Piladall in the Hargreave/Blakeley parts of Little Neston. The latter – demarked clearly in the illustration – can be accessed (with the farmer's permission!) from Hargrave House Farm: the landowner of Hargrave was once the Norseman **Ásgautr** (Chapter 17): A millenium later in 2000AD Hargrave House Farm is occupied by the **Hardings**.

The Piladall stream in Little Neston/Hargrave starts off from Mickledale at SJ343798 and moves into Raby parish where it is recorded as "Pellerdale" at approximately where the M53 motorway now runs through at SJ338795. Then on crossing the "border" as "Piledale" into the English territories of Willaston parish at SJ336791 it runs through to a pool at SJ332788. None of the names Piladall, Pellerdale or Piledale are in use now. Piladall and Pellerdale are represented in the Tithe maps, but the latest record of Piledale is only 1309. Doubtless these were all connected and the relation of these with Mickledale, Leicherichewalledale and Vilkynstane is considered in the *Cheshire Sheaf* extract above. Mickledale/Dibbinsdale itself, with its wooded valley, marks a natural boundary even without the modern barbed wire fence. The positioning of the border here is well recognised by the names Raby and Hargrave. Raby is what the Vikings called *Rá-býr* ("boundary settlement") and Hargrave is Old English for "hoary woods" - an area left unmolested as a "no-mans land" boundary (see Chapter 3). It is not clear whether Piladall forms the exact southern border since part of Raby Parish lips underneath Hargrave; also the boundary with English Willaston - defined by the ancient boundary stones "Richardston le Reve and Vilkynstane" is some 300 metres to the south of it. It is tempting to speculate whether these stones where placed by the Vikings – and whether they can possibly still be identified.

View of Willow Valley - *Piladall* - looking eastwards towards the boundary of the Norse enclave at Mickledale. Mickledale "Great Valley" is now Plymyard Dale and the stream is Dibbinsdale Brook. The large shrubby tree in the centre, on the Hargrave (left) side of the stream, is a willow. It is probably *Salix viminalis* "Osier" (or possibly *Salix caprea* or *cinerea*) - well known for its use in basket weaving. Most of the other trees in the picture appear to be Sycamore which would not have been there when the Vikings, including *Ásgautr*, arrived. The willow however is relatively close to the stream and has a large spread to it, indicating an older specimen, so it is possible that the ancestral tree was there to be used by the "locals" at the time. Willows can attain a great apparent age not by growing as one big tree, which might just reach 200 years, but by self layering and effectively growing new trees each time a branch touches the ground: in this way it can attain both huge dimensions and considerable age.

Mercifully the M53 Motorway misses the main part at Piladall, where the valley and the woodland still remain, retaining the sense of natural beauty once witnessed. Clearly a case for revival of the name? Not far from the peace and tranquility of this area, across the border in Bromborough was in stark contrast perhaps witness to one of the greatest battles in Anglo-Scandinavian history.

# Chapter 11
## ACROSS THE BORDER: ANLAF AND THE BATTLE OF BROMBOROUGH

*"In no other locality does the context of geography, politics and place-names accord so well with the few facts we possess concerning the contest"*. The Saga-Book of the Viking Society, vol XIV, part 4.

Across the border from Piladall and Raby into Bromborough parish marks the possible location of one of the most significant battles in the history between the Norwegians and the English. This occurred about two generations after the arrival of Ingimund and the first settlers: **Brunanburh, 937AD.**

The Wirral colony by then would have been well established following a quarter of a century of continuous settlement and vigorous, occasionally armed, expansion towards the wealthier English districts of the south and east. Outliers had been established from the main Wirral stronghold into South Chester and the Helsby area, and also across the shores of both the Mersey and Dee. Across the Dee, for example, Talacre is Norse. Across the Mersey at least another pair of Wirral sattellites had been established encompassing Crosby and Formby towards the west and to what is now the Wavertree/Huyton area on the eastern side of Liverpool: the latter satellite had another Thingwall and a Roby demarking, like Raby on the Wirral, the boundary. It is therefore proper to suppose that by 937AD there would have existed on either shore of both the Mersey and Dee estuaries centering on the Wirral a strong and active community of Norse settlers who would be very sympathetic to any military Norse expedition coming in or out by either estuary.

One such occurrence did apparently happen and is recorded in four sources: the Anglo Saxon Chronicle, a mid-10th century Latin poem quoted by the Norman writer William of Malmesbury, a further separate 12th century account by him and another 12th century account by a Florence or "John" of Worcester. The Icelandic saga *Egil's Saga*, written (it is thought) by Snorri Sturluson in the early 13th century, also records a battle which is named *Vínheiði* but is widely regarded as being one and the same as *Brunanburh*. The battle involved the Norseman *Anlaf* (Ólaf), aided by Constantin II, king of the Scots, against an English force led by Æthelstan and his brother Edmund. After the battle, Anlaf and the Norsemen returned by ship to Dublin across what the writers refer to as *Dingesmere*.

## The poem

The Anglo-Saxon poem, in its translated version from William of Malmesbury reads as follows (see Campbell, A. *The Battle of Brunanburh*, London 1938 and Hamer, R. A. *Choice of Anglo-Saxon Verse, Selected, with an Introduction and a Parallel verse translation*, Faber and Faber 1970)

> King Athelstan, the lord of warriors,
> Patron of heroes, and his brother too,
> Prince Edmund, won themselves eternal glory
> In battle with the edges of their swords
> Round Brunanburh; they broke the wall of shields,
> The sons of Edward with their well-forged swords
> Slashed at the linden-shields; such was their nature
> From boyhood that in battle they had often
> Fought for their land, its treasures and its homes,
> Against all enemies. Their foes fell dead,
> The Scottish soldiers and their pirate host
> Were doomed to perish; and with blood of men

The field was darkened from the time the sun
Rose at the break of day, the glorious star,
God the eternal Lord's bright candle passed
Across the land, until this noble creature
Sank to its resting-place. There many men
Lay slain by spears, and northern warriors
Shot down despite their shields, and Scotsmen too,
Weary, with battle sated. The West Saxons
Throughout the whole long passing of the day
Pressed on in troops behind the hostile people,
Hewed fiercely from the rear the fleeing host
With well-ground swords. The Mercians refused
Hard battle-play to none among the fighters
Who came with Anlaf over rolling seas,
Bringing invasion to this land by ship,
Destined to die in battle. Five young kings
Lay dead upon the battlefield, by swords
Sent to their final sleep; and likewise seven
Of Anlaf's earls, and countless of his host,
Both Scots and seamen. There the Norsemen's chief
Was put to flight, and driven by dire need
With a small retinue to seek his ship.
The ship pressed out to sea, the king departed
Onto the yellow flood and saved his life.
Likewise the wise old Constantinus came,
The veteran, to his northern native land
By flight; he had no reason to exult
In that encounter; for he lost there friends
And was deprived of kinsmen in the strife
Upon that battlefield, and left his son
Destroyed by wounds on that grim place of slaughter,
The young man in the fight. The grey-haired man
Had little cause to boast about that battle,

The sly old soldier, any more than Anlaf;
They could not with their remnant laugh and claim
That they were better in warlike deeds
When banners met upon the battlefield,
Spears clashed and heroes greeted one another,
Weapons contended, when they played at war
With Edward's sons upon the place of carnage.
The Norsemen left them in their well-nailed ships,
The sad survivors of the darts, on *Dingesmere*
Over the deep sea back they went to Dublin,
To Ireland they returned with shameful hearts.
The brothers also both went home together,
The king and prince returned to their own country,
The land of Wessex, triumphing in war.
They left behind corpses for the dark
Black-coated raven, horny beaked to enjoy,
And for the eagle, white-backed and dun-coated,
The greedy war-hawk, and that grey wild beast
The forest wolf. Nor has there on this island
Been ever yet a greater number slain,
Killed by the edges of the sword before
This time, as books make known to us, and old
And learned scholars, after hither came
The Angles and the Saxons from the east
Over the broad sea sought the land of Britain,
Proud warmakers. Victorious warriors,
Conquered the Welsh, and so obtained this land.

The closing statement recounts the Saxon conquest of what became England from the Britons (Welsh). The poem clearly originates from a Saxon, and according to him the Norsemen did not do very well here!

## Dodgson's identification of Brunanburh with Bromborough

Although none of the four English sources - nor *Egil's Saga* - pinpoints the location of Brunanburh, scholars like J. McNeal Dodgson appear to have little doubt the location was Bromborough: the interested reader is referred to *Wirral and its Viking Heritage* (Chapter 5 and pages 4, 123) and also the arguments presented in *The Place Names of Cheshire Part IV*, pages 238-239. Several reasons have been given - the battle must have taken place not far from the sea with the escape across *Dingesmere*. The existence of the strong Norse community on the Wirral and on the opposite shores of the Dee and Mersey would have provided the ideal beachhead for Norse and Norse-Irish armies coming in and getting away again, and the regular phonological development of Brunanburh would have given Bromborough. Dodgson also addresses the three possible arguments against the identification of Brunanburh as Bromborough: 1. the battlefield is referred to in the five sources by various names; 2. Florence (John) of Worcester places the landing of the Norsemen in Humber; 3. the lack of evidence about the identity of *Dingesmere*.

## In his answer to the first possible argument against

Of the other places proposed for the battle, only Burnswark in Dumfrieshire is synonymous with any of the other names in the sources – *Bruneswerce* – but this *werc* form is no more than a paraphrase of Brunanburh. The ON name *Vínheiði við Vínuskógar* in *Egil's Saga* was shown by A. Campbell in his book to be irrelevant to geography. Dodgson also points out that although the alternative names Brunandune, Brunefeld and Brunfort, which have as first element the OE pers.n. *Bruna*, do not appear among Wirral place names, analagous ones do, at Brimstage and *Brimston*, in Bromborough parish itself.

**In his answer to the second possible argument against**

Dodgson points out that even if this were true, the point of re-embarkation need not be near that of landing. The local historian Ann Anderson has dismissed the Humber as a sensible landing site for Anlaf's force coming from Dublin (see below). Page 123 of *Wirral and its Viking Heritage* also explains how Florence missed the significance of the English King Edgar visiting the Dee area in AD 973 as refreshing memories of Brunanburh to the Celts and Vikings.

**In his answer to the third possible argument against**

Dodgson points out that Dingesmere is a poetical nonce word and cannot be identified with anywhere: it is as likely to be the Dee as anywhere else. If it were discovered that this was a name for the Dee or the Irish Sea, then Bromborough's claim could be emphasised further.

**Ann Anderson's identification of Brunanburh with Bromborough**

The local historian Ann Anderson (1882 – 1969) writes the following from her privately published book on the *The Story of Bromborough* which elegantly complements Dodgson's seminal work. Her account, written in 1964, is as follows:

THE BATTLE OF BRUNANBURH (ANN ANDERSON)
Now we have a provocative subject: the site of the Battle of Brunanburh in AD 937. Bromborough is one of the forty claimants for the site.

The rival sites include places as far apart as Burnswalk in Dumfrieshire, Musbury between Axminster and Colyton, Bamber Bridge in Lancashire (in which locality the famous Cuerdale hoard of Saxon coins was found), Burnard near Barton-on-Humber and Blackburn.

This 'Waterloo' of the tenth century decided the fate of

England: whether she was to be ruled by a Saxon or a Norse king. It was such a battle as had never been seen in Britain. When at last the Saxon king drew off his victorious forces, five kings, seven earls, and thousands of men lay dead on the field.

How did this conflict arise? *Cherchez la femme*. Yes, the trouble really started over a woman. Somewhere about the year AD 915, Athelstan, the West Saxon king, gave his sister in marriage to Sithric, the Norse king of Northumbria who, on his marriage, embraced the Christian religion. Finding it, however, not so convenient as his old faith – which had allowed him to murder and pillage to his heart's content – he repented of his conversion, and got rid of his wife and his religion together. Athelstan, to avenge the honour of his sister, marched an army into Northumbria. To complicate matters, Sithric died suddenly, so Athelstan vented his wrath on Sithric's sons, Anlaf and Godfrid, whom he turned away and annexed Northumbria to his own kingdom. Anlaf fled to Dublin and Godfrid took to a mode of life always congenial to his race, namely piracy.

Anlaf, however, determined to win back his father's kingdom, formed a league with Constantine II, king of Scotland, his father-in-law, and with the Welsh and Norsemen in Northumbria and East Anglia. He also received strong contingents of warriors from the region of the Baltic, and as his own Irish forces were large, it was altogether a formidable army that Athelstan had to encounter. Now for the question: where did the battle take place?

The story is given in poetic form incorporated into the Anglo-Saxon Chronicle. The poem does not give the least indication of the locality of the engagement.

The first point to note is that Anlaf came over with his forces from Ireland, and it seems hard to understand why he should have gone pleasure cruising round the Pentland Firth to land in the Humber or somewhere on the east coast when he had estuaries like the Mersey, Dee and Ribble opposite his door.

*Wirral was a Scandinavian stronghold and he would be likely to make for a landing-place where he had friends.* Let us visualize the scene. Anlaf, with his Hiberno-Norse forces, sailed from Dublin. The Scots, probably from Clyde or Galloway, joined them off the Isle of Man, the common rendezvous. The united forces cruised along the coast of Wales to pick up their Welsh allies. Their passage up the Dee would be barred by Chester or Shotwick Castle, undoubtedly a Saxon fort.

*Wirral held friends, so what more likely than that he should land, perhaps at Wallasey, perhaps at Bromborough Pool, an ideal creek for the landing of such boats as those of Anlaf.* Thence they would march into Mercia, avoiding Chester on the one hand and Shotwick on the other, and await events.

Commanders in those days, landing on enemy territory, never liked to move far from base until they had won their footing, and Anlaf could hardly be nearer to his base at Dublin than in Wirral. Meanwhile, knowing well the storm was brewing, Athelstan had gathered together the whole of his available forces, and had encamped, if the tradition of William of Malmesbury is reliable, in the Midlands, ready to strike in whatever direction his enemy landed. If our contention is correct that Anlaf's landing place was Bromborough Pool, then Athelstan would move his men as quickly as possible to attack, for it as desirable that an invader should be intercepted before he had ravaged the country around. It was Anlaf's game to stay on the defensive just as it was Athelstan's to attack. The late Mr. Godfrey Matthews believed that the ridge of high land at Spital just above the dam, and continuing to Bidston would make an admirable defensive position for Anlaf's army; and if Brunanburh is Bromborough, there is little doubt that it was on the ridge from Spital to Higher Bebington that the battle was fought. The name 'Red Hill' or 'Bloody Hill' in that neighbourhood, supports that claim.

The Chronicle account implies that the Northmen were on the defensive:

Edward's children the shield-wall cleft

After the terrible defeat:

There put to flight was
The Northmen's chieftain
By need driven
To the ships' prow
With a little band.

These lines suggest a hurried flight to their ships and a quick embarkation. With ships anchored in the Pool at Bromborough Pool the distance would have been short.

Summarizing Bromborough's claim:

(a)   Given the existence of a Brunanburh there was but one Brunanburh in England in 937, just as there is but one Bromborough today

(b)   The Dee and Mersey whose estuaries are divided by the Wirral Peninsula have, from time immemorial, been the favourite place of embarkation to, and debarkation from, Ireland.

(c)   In the map entitled *Die Britischen Inseln* (1880) Brunanburh is placed on the 'Meresige' about the present position of Bromborough

The Saga Book of the Viking Society, vol. XIV, part 4, sums up the position thus:

*Bromborough in Wirral would appear to be the most eligible place for the battle-field. In no other locality does the context of geography, politics, and place-names accord so well with the few facts we possess concerning the contest.*

The above section by Ann Anderson was written before she had access to J. Dodgson's penetrating analysis. However, the two appear to compliment each other rather well.

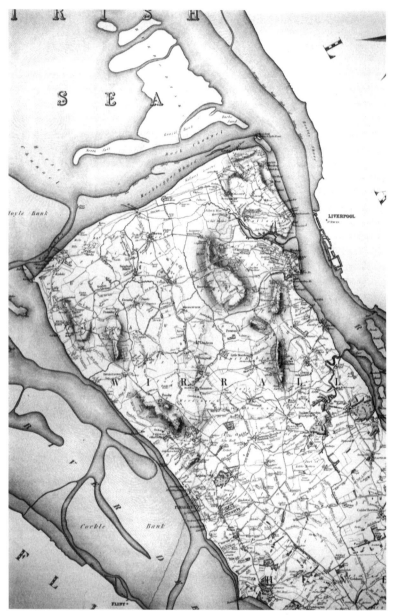

1831 map by A. Bryant of the Wirral (exluding the southernmost regions) showing the ridges of high ground running along the western and eastern sides. Courtesy of Chester & Cheshire Archives & Local Studies

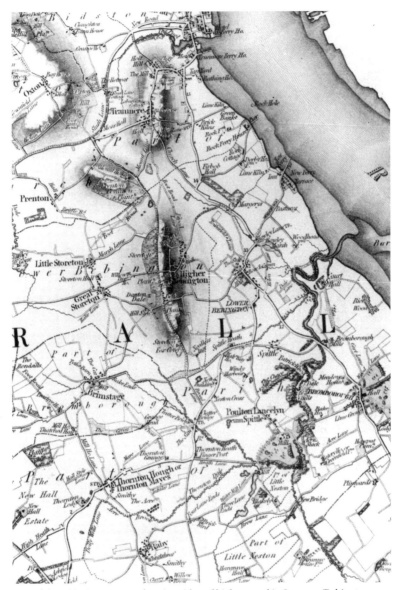

Part of the 1831 Bryant map showing ridge of high ground in Storeton/Bebington area running up to Tranmere Pool and Oxton. "Court Hall" can be seen near mouth of the Dibbin. Arno Hill (Chap. 8) is just to the south of Oxton Hill near top left-side of the map. To the south-east, between Hargrave House Farm and the Dibbin is (unmarked) Pilladall (Chap. 10). Courtesy of Chester & Cheshire Archives & Local Studies.

131

## Battle lines

As pointed out in the above passage by Ann Anderson, the battle would have extended over a wide area and along the ridge from Spital & Higher Bebington: the Wirral has two approximately parallel ridges of high ground running through it, principally sandstone based. Along the west side it forms the hills at Heswall (with a hollow at The Slack), Thurstaston (including Thorsteinn's Common) and Caldy (including The Kneckyn). Along the Eastern side it runs from Spital through to Higher Bebington/ Storeton, and then through to Oxton (including Árno Hill), Bidston and Wallasey (including the Breck): It is the southern area of this ridge, at least up to Storeton Hill, which could have represented a battle line, with presumably *Anlaf's* army towards the west and north.

A prominent area of the battle was formerly believed to have been Wargraves (see Chapter 7 and the Mainwaring map) presumably because of the unusual name. More recently the highly ditched/moated site of what used to be Bromborough Court House (off Poole Lane at SJ345842) – presumably the site also of *Bruna's* stronghold – has been considered as being a principal area in the battle. The remaining moat/ditch (as marked on Ordnance Survey maps) does not appear to be the original, as reported for example by the local archeaologist Gill Chitty: a Viking iron ring of small diameter similar to one in bronze found at Meols has been found there, discovered by a Mrs Edwards when she was living at Court House Farm: it was her son who suggested the ring was possibly medieval.

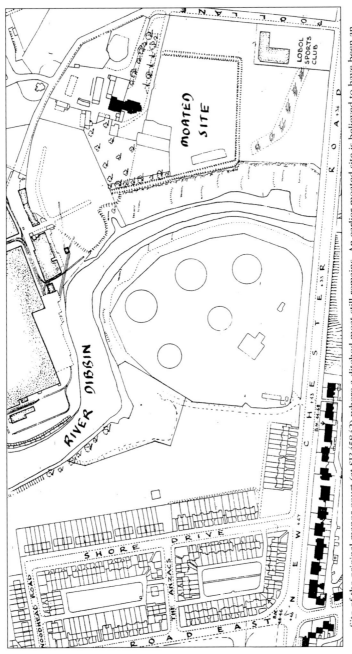

Site of the original manor court (at SJ345842) where a ditched moat still remains. An earlier moated site is believed to have been an important site of the battle of Brunanburh which would have taken place over a wide area. Courtesy of Gavin Hunter, Unilever Research, Port Sunlight

Old photograph of the Court House Farm before its demolition in 1969. From a
1948 publication "The Hardwares of Cheshire" by Roberta Glasgow,
Courtesy of Gavin Hunter

Sketch map of the boundary region between Storeton and Higher Bebington
showing Red Hill Road, "Soldiers Hill" and "Battlefields".
Based on a sketch provided by Allan Alsbury

### Red Hill Road, Soldiers Hill and Battlefields

In Ann Anderson's passage quoted above, according to local tradition a 'Red Hill' or 'Bloody Hill' along the ridge of the Storeton/Bebington boundary may have been appropriately named with reference to the battle. Further research amongst the locals has revealed an interesting collection of folklore on the matter. The local historian, Allan Alsbury, author of *Fir-Bob Land* (Countyvise, 1999) has made the following observations:

1. Local records reveal no mention of a Red Hill but **Red Hill Road** running down from the ridge (now Mount Road) towards Storeton village: it runs parallel to - and then turns north to join - "Rest Hill Road"

2. Various older residents of both Storeton and Higher Bebington (of families that have lived there for several generations) make one or more of the following points:

- Red Hill, or Red Hill Road was so named from 'the blood that once ran down it' (with reports suggesting up to 100,000 combatants were involved at Brunanburh, this is not unimaginable)
- the short, inclined length of road between the small roundabout at Storeton leading to the junction with Rest Hill and Red Hill Roads, is known as **"Soldiers' Hill"** (Area A on the illustration facing)
- lands at the side of Rest Hill Road (not precisely defined as to location) as it rises towards Mount Road ridge are known as **"Battlefields"** (Area B on the illustration)

3. A newspaper contribution, undated but almost certainly about 1955-60, with no by-line although in the style of a frequent contribtor of local history snippets of that time who generally signed as *C.R.R.* read as follows "One of the local fairy stories to which the writer was entertained as a boy was that **Kings Road** had been named after King Alfred who was thought to have fought the battle of Brunanburh in the

locality. This was, of course, not true, King being a private though prominent individual of a much later date. It was also said that King's Road had not been impoved since King Alfred's time, and this could well be true"

The latter story is clearly myth: King Alfred would have had to have risen from the grave to fight at Brunanburh – he'd been dead by almost 40 years! Nonetheless this, and the other two points do however indicate a great deal of folklore pointing to a conflict.

The illustration below gives a view from the field to the south of Red Hill Road looking up to what is now known as Prospect Hill (just above the letter B of Bracken Lane on the sketch map). The location of "Battlefields" (Area B on the map) is to the far left. Maybe the ultimate proof of Brunaburh lies beneath this soil.

Part of the ridge of high ground between Storeton and Bebington parishes. Behind the pylon on the eastern side of Mount Road is what is now Prospect Hill. Does the answer to Brunanburh lie below these fields? Does the pylon mark the thick of the battle?

**Dingesmere**

The name *Dingesmere* appearing in the poem as the waters across which what was left of Anlaf's raiding army returned to Dublin no longer exists (if it ever did). It could either have been the Dee estuary or what is now the Mockbeggar Wharf stretching along from the Viking trading port of Meols along the north Wirral coast into the Irish Sea. The Mersey estuary also cannot be ruled out with either Wallasey Pool or, as Ann Anderson has suggested, Bromborough Pool as possible docking sites. Perhaps frustratingly, the Dingesmere issue may never be resolved, and the equation Brunanburh = Bromborough may never be proved beyond any doubt. On all the other evidence we have though, the equation may well be true; some have no doubt.

**Postscript: Cherchez la femme and business as usual**

In Ann Anderson's passage she makes the interesting comment that the whole battle could be traced back to a woman – *Sithric's* saxon wife. This makes an interesting analogy to the *Harald Háfagri* story (Chapter 2) and the not insignificant part *Gyða* played leading up to the great exodus of peoples - including Ingimund - from Norway.

No doubt if, indeed, Brunanburh was Bromborough then the Scandinavian enclave in the Wirral would have lost many of its fighters: it is hard to imagine the locals not going to the assistance of their own sort. Maybe one of the "young kings" to whom the poem refers was a son or grandson of Ingimund himself. This would only however have been a temporary interruption to the steady flow of people into the enclave which continued through until well into the 11th century. "Business as usual" at the Wirral Thing...

# Chapter 12
## THE WIRRAL THING

*"It becomes obvious that in Wirral there was throughout the tenth and eleventh centuries a recognised Norse colony, deliberately established in a definitely bounded area, and with a conscious identity sufficient to support and warrant a distinctive local administration"*
J. McNeal Dodgson (1928-1990)

The local administration that the writer is referring to is the Thing at Thingwall (ON *Þingvöllr*, from *þing*=assembly and *völlr*=field, "Assembly Field"), recognised as the centre of Norse Wirral. As we have already noted earlier in the book, the Scandinavian settlers had established not long after their arrival at the start of the 10th century a community with a clearly defined border, its own leader (*Ingimundr*), its own language (Norse), a trading port (Meols) and place of assembly or government (the Thing). **This community was answerable to nobody else: neither the English, the Welsh, the Dublin Norse, the Isle of Man, Iceland, and not even Norway.** The Wirral Norse settlement therefore satisfied all the criteria of an independent, self-governing Viking State – albeit a mini one!

The Things – like the one at Thingwall - provided the method of Government throughout Norway and the Scandinavian Community. The corresponding place in Iceland, Þingvellir (*vellir*=fields, the plural of *völlr*) was used from 930AD until recently. Although the place of government in Iceland has moved from there the government is still known as the Althing (Old Norse *Alþingi* – the "All Thing") and the government in Norway at Oslo is still referred to as *"Storting"* (from Old Norse *stór-þing* "the Great Thing" – *stór*

*"Förum first bónarveg að þeim, og ef við náum þeim ekki með góðu, þá skulum við taka þá með valdi"*

Another view of the site of the Wirral Thing at Cross Hill, Thingwall. Here the Wirral Norse leader Ingimund is reported as having said the following, in connection with a confrontation with the English over lands at Chester (translation into Icelandic courtesy of Eyrún Hafsteinsdóttir and Jón Baldvinsson): *"Förum first bónarveg að þeim, og ef við náum þeim ekki með góðu, þá skulum við taka þá með valdi"* "Let us beseech and implore them first, and if we do not get them willingly in this way let us contest them by force".

Thingvellir in Iceland, Meeting place of the Icelandic Althing.Picture taken at Almannagja. Besides its extreme historical importance, it is also of considerable geological interest:The cliffs are volcanic lava. On one side is Europe and the other is America: this place is the only place in the world where you can see continental plates drifting apart. Picture courtesy of Ragnar Th. Sigurðsson.

*Ingimund's Saga*

is the same element in Wirral's Storeton). The precise location of the Wirral Thing – whose antiquity would have dated from shortly after Ingimund's arrival in 902AD or thereabouts – is believed to have been at Cross Hill, across the Barnston Road from the Reservoir. The Wirral Thing easily pre-dates the Iceland *Alþingi* and also one at Isle of Man.

The purpose of a Thing was to assemble representative people from the community to decide on matters of adminstration, policy (including military) and law. Popular codes of law used by the Norsemen were the "Grey-Goose code" (*Grágás*) originating from the Trondheim area from King Magnus the Good, son of Ólaf the Saint (see Chapter 9) - an area from where Ingimund may have originated. It is thus probable that the Wirral Thing had a similar legal code to Grey-Goose, a code which was also used by the Icelanders. Also important was the "Bjarkø law": this was a special law governing commercial and mercantile affairs and was at one time accepted as a kind of international law. International trade through Scandinavian Wirral's port at Meols would also have been regulated by the Thing.

Throughout the Viking world there were two types of Thing – the district or **Fylkis-thing** which was equivalent to local government with limited powers and answerable to higher authorities, and the central or **Lögthing** (or "Logthing") which had far reaching powers at national or regional level. The Althing "All-thing" at Thingvellir, Iceland, and the Storting at Oslo are both examples of a Lögthing or Central Thing.

Although clearly not of the same same magnitude as the Icelandic Althing, nonetheless the independent Wirral Thing may have represented not only the main Wirral settlement but also after its expansion the outliers such as at Helsby, Whitby, the Handbridge area of South Chester, the Talacre area across the Dee and the Crosby/Formby and Wavertree areas across the Mersey. And, as noted in Chapter 11, the Wavertree outlier was sufficiently remote from the main Wirral Norse enclave to have justified its own Thing – probably a Fylkis-thing at another Thingwall there.

The Wirral Thing could well have represented the interests of Norsemen scattered further afield from the Wirral centre such as Cumbria where there are Norse place names scattered over a wide area. The local historian G. Dawson wrote in his book *Tingvelle*: "it is recorded that in the year 910AD forty Viking ships anchored in Wallasey Pool for the meeting of the Thingwall parliament", although the source of this report is unclear.

The Lögthings were so powerful they would even influence the choice of monarch or leader: succession to the throne or leadership depended on a combination of hereditary and elective principles: the king had not only to be a member of the royal dynasty but also had to be accepted by the people at the Things. Ingimund himself would have been chosen following this process during a meeting of a Thing in Dublin or back home in Norway, and the Wirral Thing would have decided on his successor(s). Logthings also dealt with disputes between leaders of different regions: the district Fylkis-things were not equipped to do this. The Wirral Thing, like the others, would have scheduled meetings once or twice yearly, and also when emergencies arose – such as Brunanburh in 937AD. We know from Snorri's *Heimskringla* (History of the Kings of Norway) of several other Things in Norway between the 9th and 12th Centuries[12] :

---

[12] The interested reader can find a geographical description and distribution of the Logthings in Einar Haugen's 1976 book *The Scandinavian Languages*

## Norwegian Things

The following were examples of Logthings in Norway, as recorded in *Heimskringla*:

- **The Eyrathing or Örething** (at Niðaros, Trondheim the old Norwegian capital). This later moved to the Frosta Thing
- **The Frosta Thing** (Trondheimsfjord). The Frosta Thing's laws were established by Hákon the Good, Harald Hárfagri's son.
- **The Eidsiva Thing** (*Heiðsævisþing*). Hamar, at Heiðsævi - Lake Mjøsen. This Thing later moved further south to Eidsvöll). The Eidsiva Thing Laws – Heiðsævislög - were established by Hálfdan the Black, father of Harald Hárfagri. The Eidsiva Thing was also visited by Harald Hárfagri.
- **The Gula Thing** (western Norway). The Gula Thing's laws were also established by King Hákon the Good.
- **The Borgar-Thing** (Borg, Sarpsborg) – 50 miles south of Oslo on the east side of Oslofjord

The following were some of the many **Fylkis-things** in Norway, as recorded in *Heimskringla*: Arnaness Thing, Kefsisey Thing (Lofoten Islands – see Chapter 2), Hrafnista Thing (now Ramstad in Namdal) and the Unarheimr Thing.

## Other Things

In Denmark there was the **Viborg Thing** (Viborg is an ancient town in north Jutland). Elsewhere in the Norse commonwealth there was the **Logthing** in the Faroe Islands, **Law Ting Holm** in Shetland, **Tingwall** in the Orkneys, the Thing at **Dingwall** in North Scotland, **Tinwald** in the Scottish border area and **Tynwald** in the Isle of Man – which still meets every 5th July.

Besides the regular meetings and emergency meetings of the Things, they were also held on special occasions such as the "**Gangdagaþing**", a Thing held in the precession days of the

Lake Mjøsen/Hamar in Norway, near the site of the Eidsiva Thing - visited by *Harald Hárfagri.*The "Viking ship" stadium constructed for the 1994 Winter Olympics is in the foreground. Photograph Courtesy of Heidi Lervold, Aune-Forlag, Trondheim

Ascension week, two weeks before Whitsuntide. Snorri in his *Heimskringla* records two such, one at *Hamarsfjörður* (1st June, 1139AD) and one at *Unarheimr* (now Onareim on the island of Tysnes, Sunnhordland).

Another form of a thing was a **mót** (a Thing meeting in a town or township). One of these forms an element in the now lost place name in Storeton parish **le Gremotehalland** (last recorded 1330) which comes from Old Norse *griða-mót* meaning "place of a meeting under a truce". Just as with *le Dedemonnes Greue* (1323) – "dead man's wood" – also in Storeton, and *Lathegestfeld* (1412), of which one interpretation[13] of its meaning has been "unwelcome guest's field" in Bromborough – it possibly relates to difficulties or other types of interaction between the Norse and the surrounding English communities.

---

[13] see page 81 for a discussion on this

# Chapter 13
## THE KIRKS – CHRISTIAN VIKINGS

*"It is the popular belief that wherever the Norse came they destroyed the churches. But by the time of their settlement - here about 900AD - they had become Christianized to some extent".* William Gershom Collingwood, Germanic Historian (1854 - 1932)

It is true that most people associate the Vikings with destruction when in reality many used violence only when they had to. They were also constantly referred to by English writers – up until at least the last century – as "Heathen". The Wirral Norse population – especially those from Ireland – had in reality been Christianized "to some extent" before their arrival in Wirral in 902AD. It is therefore not surprising that they brought with them at least two churches dedicated to a Gaelic Saint and constructed an array of monuments and carvings dating from the middle of the tenth century onward. With Norse place-names and other hints of similar origin also involved, we can hardly doubt that these were the chapels of Christian 'Vikings' who had brought their religion with them from Ireland.

### Transition period
The religious situation during the early settlement period would probably have been similar to that in Iceland up to the period when Christianity was officially adopted – through compromise and consensus - by the *Alþingi* at Thingvellir in the year 1000: before then Christianity made converts whilst warily coexisting with the old pagan beliefs, as considered in the *Kristni saga*. One would imagine this to be the same position in the Wirral at least in the earlier part of the 10th century. This would be a society where the Christian priests

and the corresponding pagan *goði* or (plural) *goðar* would excerise mutual toleration until the Christian faith had become completely adopted.

## Norse-Irish churches

The two Norse churches dedicated to a Gaelic Saint at West Kirby and the Norse-Wirral outlier at Handbridge are both to St. Bridget of Ireland (450-525 AD). Another later Norse Church in the Handbridge outlier (St. Olave's) is dedicated to Ólaf the Saint, or King Ólaf Haraldsson (995-1030AD). Because of the important role both these people played – one Irish, the other Norwegian – in the religion of the area we consider now both in a little detail.

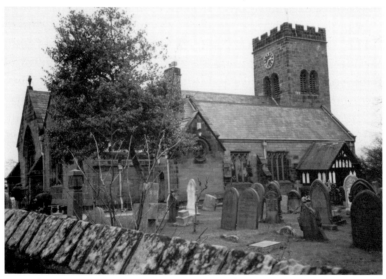

St. Bridget's West Kirby. Believed to have been founded by the Norsemen after their arrival from Ireland and named after the Irish Patron Saint. The original church was wooden. Photograph courtesy of Revd. Roger Clarke.

**St. Bridget**

St. Bridget of Ireland (not to be confused with Bridget, patron saint of Sweden who lived from 1303 to 1373) is more popularly referred to in Ireland as St. Brigid. She is, together with St. Patrick, joint Patron Saint of Ireland. She was born at Faughart, Ulster and both her parents were baptised by St. Patrick, with whom she developed a close friendship. She founded a school of art at Kildare and its illuminated manuscripts became famous, notably the Book of Kildare, which was praised as one of the finest of all illuminated Irish manuscripts. Brigid was one of the most remarkable women of her times, and demonstrated extraordinary spirituality, charity, and compassion for those in distress. Legend also attributed many miracles to her. She died at Kildare on February 1 525AD (marked by a feast day) and was buried at Downpatrick, Ireland with St. Patrick and St. Columba – the interested reader can find more about her on the Website http://catholic.org/saints/saints/ brigidireland.html. Besides in Wirral and Ireland there are many churches elsewhere dedicated to her, including London (St. Bride's, Fleet Street), West Cumberland, the Hebrides and even some in Germany. The following is a prayer from her Feast Day:

"O God, Who dost this day gladden us by the yearly festival of blessed Brigid Thy Virgin, mercifully grant that we may be helped by the merits of her whose example of chastity shines upon us with such lustre. Through our Lord".

It is worth mentioning also that according to local folklore St. Patrick himself once visited Wirral, a legend associated with St. Patrick's Well at SJ346829 in Bromborough.

**Ólaf the Saint (Olav)**

King Ólaf the Saint was responsible for making Norway a Christian country. His predecessor Ólaf Tryggvason – whose

statue stands proud in modern day Trondheim – is credited
with starting the process, but Ólaf the Saint, like Tryggvason
secured, after many years struggle, the christianisation of the
whole of Norway, including the inner regions which were
clinging on to the old beliefs of Thór, Óðinn and Valhalla. He is
credited with the saying 'let the sword pave way for the cross'.
This he achieved by 1024, where at a Thing on the island of
Moster, Christianity was accepted as the official faith in
Norway. His power in Norway diminished with the growing
power of King Canute in Denmark who had secured England
and had by 1028AD effectively taken control of Norway too,
with Earl Hákon as his overlord. Ólaf died in battle on 29th July
1030.   Shortly after his death, Ólaf was officially declared a
Saint in Trondheim and his Christian Law was soon accepted
by all in Norway. The 29th July is marked in the Norwegian
calendar as *Olsok*, Ólaf's vigil: the interested can view the Web
page http://viking.no/e/people/st.olav/e-olav.htm.

**Places with kirk**
The Wirral settlers, besides constructing their own churches,
also used existing Anglian churches, and did not destroy but
preserved them. The existence of these and other churches of
their own are revealed by major place names as well as
numerous names of roads and neighbouring fields which bear
the element *kirkja* (church). The major place names bearing
Norse church elements are:

- Kirkjubýr í Waleya "village of the Church in Wallasey" – now
  Wallasey Village, and presumably refers to the former saxon
  church at St. Hilary's Brow
- West Kirby "the west village of the church", the church
  being St. Bridgets
- Wodekirkja – now Woodchurch, which refers to a wooden
  church at the site were Holy Cross Church now is.

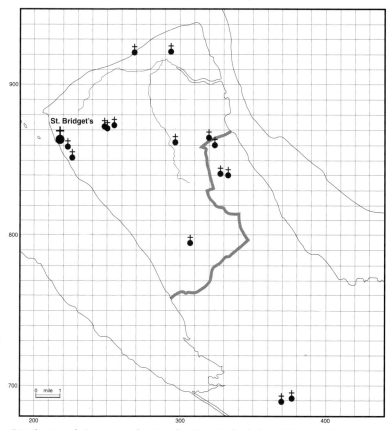

Distribution of place names bearing the element the kirk or Bridget in Wirral. From
Old Norse *kirkja* ("church") and the Irish patron saint

Inside the Wirral Norse enclave, the minor places revealing the
proximity of churches are Kyrke Cross (now lost) in Caldy
parish, Kirkeway (not the modern Kirkway!), Kirka Loons and
Top Kirka Loons in Greasby, Overkirk Hill near Overchurch
School, Kirk Hay in Prenton, Kirkett Hey in Raby, another
Kirkett Hay in Tranmere, Kirkway in Wallasey, and Kirbymount
in West Kirby. Outside the main enclave in the southern and
eastern parts of Wirral we have Kirket Lane in Lower
Bebington and Kirkland House and Kirks Field in Little

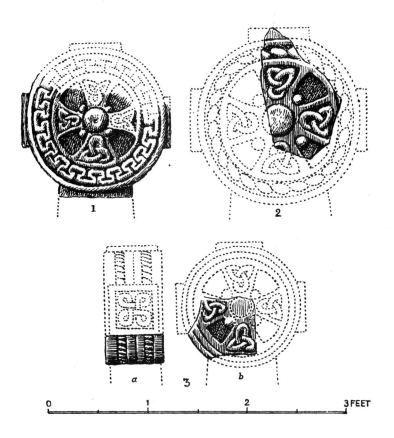

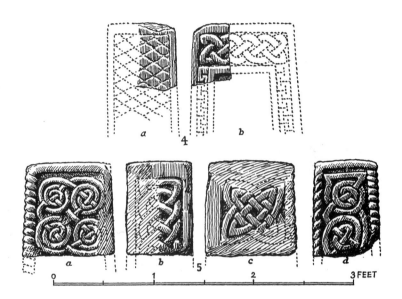

Norse Crosses at West Kirby. Drawings from W.G. Collingwood. In these sketches from 1928, Collingwood has used dotted line projections to estimate the original complete form.

1: Cross-head (red sandstone) apparently found at Hilbre in 1852. Now in Grosvenor museum, Chester;

2: Fragment of cross head (red sandstone), in the museum at West Kirby

3: Another fragment (red sandstone) in the museum at West Kirby (a) side view (b) front view;

4: Cross-shaft (red-sandstone, found 1893), in the museum at West Kirby. 11th Century, thought to be from the time of King Canute. Two adjacent sides shown;

5: Another red-sandstone cross-shaft in West Kirby from the same time. All four sides shown

Saughall. In Eastham parish there are also three field names bearing the name of Bridget: Bridgets, Nearer Bridgets and Big Bridgets.

The most remarkable church was St. Bridgets at West Kirby: it was here a number of stone crosses from the Norseman could be found together with the famous Hogback tombstone. Collingwood wrote:

"From the absence of any stones of the tenth century we may infer that the St. Bridget's of the Norse was rather a poor church in rude surroundings. Stone monuments are not made until there is well-being and until circumstances permit the growth of artistic taste. This did not come about at West Kirby until King Knút's time, and then perhaps the demand was created by the supply. There was someone at Chester who was making fine crosses; his fame reached West Kirby and people there wished to be in fashion. They sent for him and he made them examples of his best work".

So the crosses probably date from King Canute's time in the mid-11th Century (four to five generations after Ingimund).

The hogback or "recumbent" Norse tombstone is also believed to have been produced in this period. Collingwood in his article reproduced in *Wirral and its Viking Heritage* gives a full description of the tombstone and its relation to others of the period. The stone from which it was produced was originally thought to have come from Storeton, although the source that subsequently appeared to be favoured by geologists is the sandstone from the Upper Coal Measures near Ruabon and Cefn. If it had indeed come from outside the area this adds further testimony to the importance of the person whose grave it once stood by. The tombstone now resides inside St. Bridgets church after being beautifully restored in 1999 by the Merseyside Conservation Centre.

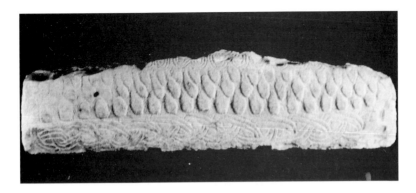

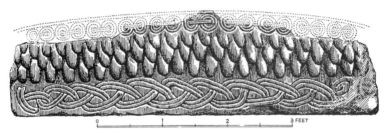

Hogback tombstone at St. Bridget's Church, West Kirby.

(a) Photograph of the front, taken in 1999 after restoration by the Merseyside Conservation Centre

(b) drawing of W.G. Collingwood of the front, as published in 1928: dotted line projections illustrate the likely form of the once intact stone

(c) 1999 photograph of the back

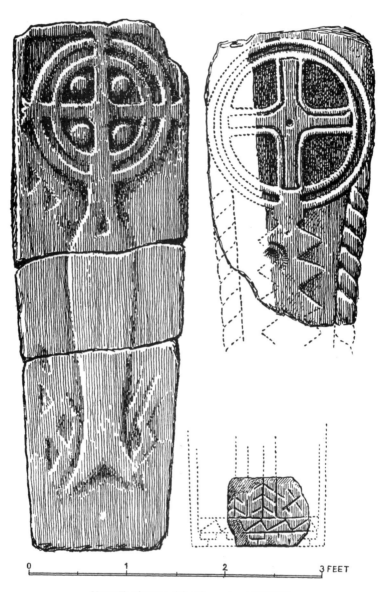

Norse Tombstone slabs (from about 1100AD).
Left: found 1864 at Hilbre;
Top right: rusticated slab fragment;
Bottom right: slab at West Kirby.
1928 sketches at West Kirby museum by W.G. Collingwood.

156

Some fifty or so years later (c.1100 AD) there was a renewed desire for tombstones and, according to Collingwood, this time the West Kirby people had among them a 'smith' who could make the kind of thing which then satisfied their Norse cousins in Galloway and elsewhere. To this smith is attributed the tombstone slabs at Hilbre and another slab at West Kirby. To the same smith has also been attributed the first stone church form of St. Bridgets from which fragments of architectural detail still remain in the existing church. Detailed descriptions of all the monuments mentioned here and the other Norse monuments found on the Wirral given by both Collingwood and J.D. Bu'Lock are reprinted in *Wirral and its Viking Heritage.*

So the heroic early-Viking tradition of burning their dead by putting their bodies on a boat, engulfing it in flames and then pushing it out to sea seems to have been replaced by Christian burial methods. By the eleventh and tweflth centuries the Wirral Norsemen were all Christian. The next question: what did these Christian Vikings do for recreation?

# Chapter 14
## BEAUTY SPOTS, HORSE RACING AND ROCK CLIMBING

*"I gripped the icy clints of the granite rock tighter".*
Sir Walter Scott (1771- 1832) in *The Raiders*

Recreation: so what did the Wirral Vikings do in their spare time? Although Tranmere existed, Tranmere Rovers association football club was not then available, but there were other opportunities on offer. On rainy days, and just like back home in Norway during the long, cold winter nights, they may have stayed inside and played the game *hnefa-tafl*, known in English as "King's Table", "Tablut" or "Jet", This game dates back to before 400AD and is a forerunner of chess and *skák-tafl* ("check table") introduced in the 11<sup>th</sup>/12<sup>th</sup> centuries. An original pair of hnefatafl pieces is currently at Warrington Museum and shown in the illustration. *Hnefa-tafl* means "head-piece table or board", where the *hnefi* has to break out of the centre of the board and avoid being surrounded by his opponents pieces: a web site where you can play this game on-line is given at the end of the book. Describing the main *hnefi* piece the museum writes the following: "Jet figure with bevelled edges, ornamented with scratched lines and circles, possibly drawn with an instrument such as a compass". Of the other piece "Jet figure: cylindrical with bevelled top". The drawing pin is included to give an idea of size.

For outdoor pursuits the Wirral Norse could visit the many beauty spots in the area, or race their horses at the two Viking race tracks, or even –young or old - practice their rock climbing skills.

*Hnefatafl* ("Tablut") pieces (c. 10th Century) now at Warrington Museum. Courtesy of Angela Doyle and Keith Scott

## Beauty spots: Raby Mere

We have already referred to the location of beauty spots at **Piladall** "Willow Valley" in the border area (illustrated in Chapter 10) – if the Vikings were partial to a picnic then this would be one of a number of attractive areas. One of these would have been nearby Raby Mere (at SJ330810), also right near the border (*rá-býr*: ON "boundary settlement") with "English" Poulton. Ann Anderson, whom we quoted in Chapter 11 about Brunanburh, wrote the following about Raby Mere in her 1964 book on the *Story of Bromborough*:

RABY MERE (ANN ANDERSON)

Raby Mere is a beautiful sheet of water about a mile-and-a-half from Bromborough. It is surrounded by woodland and is at its loveliest in May when masses of bluebells cover hill and valley and provide a wonderful eye-catcher, while boats on the mere give quiet recreation. The walk to Raby Mere from Bromborough is one of sheer delight. First, the quiet woodland dell, then the smooth grassy hill slopes, next the fruitful cornfields and at last the romantic sunken lane leading direct to the Mere. The connection of *Raby* with Norse settlers is provided by the name, which means 'boundary'. This is further emphasized by a field name **'Twizzle-Hey'**. The Norse word *Twistle* means boundary also. The field so named lies not only on the boundary where Raby joins Willaston, but at the boundary also of two estates.

Raby is linked with Brimstage (Brunstath, the old Norse form for 'The place of Brun') which was the ancient settlement of the Domvilles, a house of high consideration among the gentry of Cheshire; most probably a junior branch of the Barons of Montalt. Through the marriage of heiresses the estates of the Hulses, Rabys, Domvilles and several other families passed into the hands of the Earls of Shrewsbury. The Talbot coat-of-arms, though much defaced, was quite decipherable on Raby water-mill. The old water-mill has been demolished, but its date stone inscribed W I 1791' has been set in a garden wall overlooking the Mere. Earlier date-stones have disappeared... The charming mill-house still stands and serves tea to stray visitors in its romantic little garden.

It is impossible to speculate whether the Wirral Norse used this area for similar purposes but we do know that the stepping stones at Raby Mill are ancient. The part forming the border with Poulton-cum-Spital has the following ancient name recorded in the Parish records for Poulton **"La Stopelrake"** which means "the lane or path to the stepping stones", with ON *rák*, so the stepping stones were most likely there back in the times of the early Norse settlers.

Raby Mere: near the "border" with Poulton

## Other beauty spots

It is possible from a perusal of the complete list of Viking place names (Chapters 6, 7) to identify where some of the other likely places of particular natural beauty were:

- Ascow (*Askrskógr*) in Caldy: "Ash Wood" – probably somewhere near SJ234845
- Vfeldesgrene in Claughton:"Úfaldi's Green or Wood" – there are no problems finding this because it is now, or at least forms part of, Birkenhead Park
- Arno Hill or "The Arno" in Oxton:"Árni's Hill" – where there must have been excellent views, at SJ305872
- Cross Hill in Thingwall – site of the Thing, but where there also must have been excellent views, now partially obscured by the reservoir on the opposite side of Barnston Road, at SJ281844

- Steyncolesdale (*Steinkeldalr*) "Steinkell's valley", from SJ240829 to SJ241831 and Thurstaston (Þorsteinn's) Common in Thurstaston
- Asker Dale (*Askrdalr*) "Ash-tree valley" at Tranmere, at SJ327877

The locations of all these, together with Raby Mere and Piladall/Pellerdale/Piledale, are indicated by a picnic table symbol in the illustration below. For those who liked to be near some water there would have been:

- Ragnhildr's Pool and Gunnhildr's Pool, also at Tranmere, from SJ330882 to SJ322885 and at SJ330872 respectively. Both pools have now gone
- Ketilspol – Ketill's creek at Hooton (now Riveacre Country Park) at SJ379779
- Ingriesicche: Ingríðr's stream at Capenhurst, possibly near SJ370735

Also on the outskirts of Chester - like Ingríðr's stream - the Wirral Vikings could visit Grymisgreue (Grímr or Óðinn's Wood) probably near SJ344722 at Woodbank. *Grímr* was a by-word for the most important Norse god, Óðinn. It was also a personal name: the same name appears in a list of pre-Domesday landowners from the area (see Chapter 17). For those wishing to retrace the steps of these early Wirral settlers the locations of all these places are given in Chapters 6 and 7.

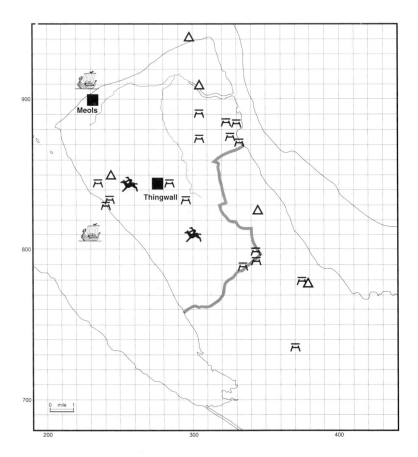

Viking Recreation
⊼ : beauty spots;
⊁ : *Hesta-skeið* (Heskeths – horse race tracks);
△ : klintir (including Thór's Stone, the large rock at Wallasey Breck & Red Noses).
Also shown are Thingwall (the main site of government) and Meols
(the main seaport).

### Viking Horse Racing at Irby and Thornton Hough

For the sportsmen, horse racing was evidently popular with apparently at least two race tracks, one at *Hestaskeið* (Heskeths) in Irby and another *Hestaskeið* at Thornton Hough. It is perhaps significant that one of these race tracks is at Irby – "settlement of the Irish" - and perhaps reflects the great love of horse racing seen today in modern day Ireland.

The location of the former Irby race track - as identified as "Heskeths" from the Parish Tithe map - is the field lying between Woodlands Road and Thingwall Road. The other Hestaskeið in Thornton Hough is recorded in the 1843 Tithe apportionment as Hesketh Grange.

Heskeths in Irby. Horse race-track *(hestaskeið)* for the Vikings at SJ257844 seen from the bottom of Woodlands Road at Arrowe Brook looking towards Thingwall Road.

The tradition of horse racing in the Wirral extended throughout the middle ages and culminated in the construction of a new *hestaskeið* by the 16th Century Earl of Derby in the grounds of the newly constructed Leasowe Castle at Wallasey (the grounds of the Castle provided also the legendary site of Canute's Chair – Chapter 16): this was the location of the first "Derby races" before their later transfer to Newmarket and then Epsom.

### Rock climbing at the klintir

Coming from mountainous Norway the settlers no doubt would have been tempted to try their hand at climbing the various *klintir* (Old Norse for "projecting rocks" or "tough stone"). Although there are no mountains in the Wirral the several *klintir* would have presented an interesting challenge particularly for the youngsters. This tradition of rock climbing also persisted right through the middle ages and was not without its hazards.

Two articles in the *Cheshire Sheaf* - the first written by a "Holly of Liverpool" in 1898 and followed by a reply - also in 1898 - from William Fergusson Irvine of Birkenhead recall a 17th century entry in the Wallasey Parish records concerning the Clynsse (*klint/klintir*) at Wallasey in relation to the unfortunate death in 1642 of two people - Elizabeth Smyth and May Johnson - who either fell while climbing or were hit by something falling off one of these *klintir*. One of the proposed sites for this accident was the Red-Noses "Clint" near the mouth of the Mersey estuary, the other being the "Clint" at the Breck (*brekka* - itself a Norse word meaning "slope, hillside") in Wallasey Village. The latter is clearly the more awe-inspiring and is probably the likelier site of the accident.

FROM CHESHIRE SHEAF, VOL. 2, MARCH 1898, PAGE 35. EXTRACT FROM ARTICLE 184: A CURIOUS ENTRY IN THE WALLASEY PARISH REGISTER
Under date 1642 is the following curious entry among the burials: - "Elizabeth Smyth and May Johnson kild at ye Clynsse (*klintir*) by a fall of a pinacle on ye 24th of June were buried on ye 27th June". Can any readers suggest an explanation of 'ye Clinsse?'.... Halliwell gives: 'Clints, crevices among bare limestone rocks (North country).'

There are, of course, no limestone rocks in Wallasey, but it might be used as referring to the clefts or steep gullies in the sandstone rocks on The Breck, or even at the Red Noses near the modern New Brighton; but even if this were so, it is difficult to see where 'the pinnacle' would come from, unless the word is used as descriptive of loose points of stone standing on the edge of the rock, which might have fallen and killed the women. Any suggestion would be welcome. Yours, *Holly*, Liverpool.

REPLY: ARTICLE 275, PAGE 96 (AUGUST 1898): A CURIOUS ENTRY IN THE WALLASEY PARISH REGISTER
The following extract from the Dialect Dictionary may throw light on the obscure entry in the Wallasey Register: -
CLINT.    1.  A rocky cliff, a projecting rock or ledge
          2.  Hard or flinty rocks: a species of limestone or porphoryte stone.
          3.  A hard tough stone used in the game of curling
          4.  A crevice among bare limestone rocks

A quotation is made from *The Raiders*: "I gripped the icy clints of the granite rock tighter". From this it will be seen that the probable meaning of 'The Clints' in the extract from the Register, should be rocky ledges or cliffs, so that the two women must have been killed by a fall of stone on some rocky point in Wallasey, probably the Breck near the Church, though it may have been at the Red Noses. It would be interesting to find if any trace of this place name still exists. Yours, &c., *William Fergusson Irvine*, Birkenhead.

The "Raiders" Fergusson Irvine refers to here is a novel by Walter Scott. I myself climbed the Clint at the Wallasey Breck many times as a youngster in the 1960's and it is considerably more challenging than the Red Noses! Concerning the latter, on the old photograph over the page (top), it is possible to make-out someone climbing the right hand rock face.

The Wallasey *klintir*: Top, the klintir at Red Noses, New Brighton SJ298942. Bottom: The klint at Wallasey Breck, SJ305908. The photographs, from the early 1900's {a group having a picnic are just visible behind the left hand "Red Nose" with somebody climbing the right hand one} are courtesy of Wallasey Central Reference Library.

Another interesting set of *klintir* can be found at what is now Brotherton Park, Bromborough, situated on the southern bank of the River Dibbin at SJ345826 & SJ345827.

The Bromborough *klintir* (partially hidden by the trees, just above the pathway) at Brotherton Park. Photograph taken from a fallen tree stretching across the R. Dibbin

Besides projecting rocks the Norse word *klintir* was also used for "tough stones": for example, the enthusiast looking for projecting rocks for the Little Sutton *klintir* will soon become frustrated – however he will find identifiable tough stones (SJ371776) which appear to fit the description at the golf course there.

The most famous *klintir* in the Wirral is however without question the magnificient *Þórr Mjöllnir* (Thór's hammer or stone at Thurstaston) which represents such an important part of Wirral folklore and tradition that it deserves a separate chapter by itself.

# Chapter 15
## THÓR

*"This record of Danish heathendom...the gigantic rock altar"*
Sir James Allanson Picton, Liverpool Antiquarian (1805-1889)

A crack of thunder and you can hear Thór's anger... It is easy to dismiss the above statement about Thór's Stone at Thurstaston by one of Merseyside's most famous Victorian antiquarians: the Wirral population to whom this is attributed were neither Danish - apart from a relatively small minority based probably around Denhall - nor generally "heathen": they were mostly Norwegian (with some Irish) and probably mostly Christianized by the time they settled in the 10th century. However, there is a belief – firmly entrenched in Wirral folklore - that Thór's Stone, a most impressive giant rocky outcrop in the midst of the sandstone based Thurstaton Hill & Common is actually the final resting place of *Mjöllnir*, the hammer of the Norse god of thunder, Thór, shown protecting the world by fighting the Frost Giant ogres in the illustration on page 172.

There is no reason to reject completely the view of local folklore that this tradition dates right back to the time of the settlements. Although largely Christian, all the settlers would still have brought with them their traditions and stories about the Norse gods, as later described in Snorri Sturlusons *Prose Edda* and set beautifully to music by Wagner in the *Ring*. In fact Picton's statement had built on a tradition which goes back much further: as to how far back – three, 10, 30, or the 40 generations - to the original colonialists we shall never know.

Thór, with his chariot, his goats and hammer *Mjöllnir*, confronting the Frost Giants. 1872 painting by Mårtin Eskil Winge. Reproduced courtesy of the Swedish National Museum, Stockholm

*Mjöllnir*: Thór's Stone, Thurstaston, at SJ244849. Like the *klintir* at the Wallasey Breck and Red Noses, a popular climbing spot for young and old. The photograph shows Thomas (12) and Matthew (17) Harding, the latter sporting a Tranmere FC shirt: the uniform of the modern day Wirral Viking!

*Ingimund's Saga*

The Norse god Thór (Old Norse *Þórr*, German Donner), gives his name to Thursday. In Norway it is Torsdag, in Germany Donnerstag. Interestingly the Icelanders stopped naming their days after Norse gods following a religious clampdown and Thursday is *fimmtudagur* ("5th Day"). Other gods giving their names to days are *Týr* (Tuesday, in Norway *Tirsdag*), *Oðinn* (Wednesday, *Onsdag*), *Freyr* (Friday, *Freidag*). The *Prose Edda* says the following (translation by Jean Young):

'Thór, who is called Ása-Thór or Thór-the-charioteer, is the foremost of the gods other than Óðinn, and was generally the most popular amongst the Norse peoples. He is strongest of all gods and men and protects the world against giants and frost ogres. He rules over that kingdom called *Thrúðvangar* ("Plains-of-power") and his hall is called *Bilskirnir* ("Strong"); in that building are six hundred and forty floors – it is the largest house known to men... Thór has two goats known as Tooth-gnasher and Gap-tooth, and the chariot he drives in, and the goats pull the chariot, and for this reason he is called Thór-the-charioteer. He also owns three precious things. One is the hammer *Mjöllnir* ("Crusher"), which the frost ogres and cliff giants know when it is rasied aloft. His second great treasure is a belt of strength, and when he buckles that on his divine might is doubled. And he owns a third thing of great value in his iron gauntlets; he cannot do without these when he grips the handle of the hammer. But no one is well-informed enough to be able to recount all his mighty deeds"

The rock itself is as daunting as the *klintir* at the Wallasey Breck (Chapter 14) and is certainly befitting of *Mjöllnir*. It also a popular climbing spot amongst young and old alike.

N.F. "Nomad" Ellison – the once widely known Wirral writer wrote in his 1955 book:

"The mecca of those who visit Thurstaston' is Thór's Stone, a huge isolated block of red sandstone, roughly 50 feet (17m) in length, 30 feet (10m) wide and 25 feet (8m) high, standing in a natural amphitheatre whose sloping sides are aglow in the late summer with the rich purples of heather and ling".

He goes on to point out that it was possibly the harder rock which caps the hill - and not Thór's Stone itself - which had been the subject of intense human labour, quarried for walls and buildings, leaving Thór's Stone untouched: time and weathering has given it the more rounded shape we see today. Its atmosphere and awe is there for all to see.

Even today it attracts "Viking" style marriages from groups such as the "Sons of Odin" – as the occasional local paper articles testify. Daybreak of May 1st does see a pagan ritual in the form of Morris Dancing to give good fortune for the summer ahead.

But it was the Victorians who let their imaginations flow. Immediately prior to the Victorian age a frequent visitor to the Wirral, and staying in the newly built Stanley Hotel in Hoylake in the latter part of the 18th century, was the poet Anna Seward, friend of Sir Walter Scott, the author of *The Raiders* – see the previous chapter. Besides being much sought after by the gentlemen of the day she was one of the early people to realise the significance of the Wirral in Norse History, and her visits inspired her to produce draft verse paraphrases of two Viking Age poems, namely *Herva, at the Tomb of Argantyr* and *Harold's Complaint. A Scandinavian Ode.*

Morris Dancing, May 1st at Thór's Stone. From Wirral News, 3 May 2000. John Foster, Morris Dancer Squire:"We dance at Thór's Stone because it's a very atmospheric place steeped in history". Reproduced, courtesy of Wirral Newspapers

Anna Seward, poet, 1747-1809. Courtesy of Peter Young, Lichfield City Council

The most prominent of the Victorians was, however, Sir James Picton who, as alluded to above, propagated in lectures and also in writings in the journal *Notes and Queries* (1881, 1885) the story that the rock was once used by the Vikings as a sacrificial altar in honour of Thór. Picton was not alone. P. Sulley in his books *The Hundred of the Wirral* (Birkenhead 1889) and *History of Ancient and Modern Birkenhead*, (Murphy, Liverpool, 1907) wrote "the great stone of Thór was reddened with the blood of priests and captives". Hilda Gamlin who wrote the books *Memories/The Chronicles of Birkenhead: the Scenes and People of its Early Days*, (Holwell, Liverpool, 1892) and *'Twixt Mersey and Dee'*, Marples, (Liverpool, 1897) made the fascinating connection with the battle of Brunanburh:

Sir James Picton, Victorian antiquarian, 1805-1889. Photograph courtesy of the
Picton Reference Library, Liverpool

"the stone was probably raised by the Danes to commemorate the great battle of Brunenburh".

Hilda Gamlin - like Picton - mistakenly refers to the Wirral Norse settlers as Danes. This is a fault of neither of these writers but a reflection of an English tradition dating back to Saxon times to regard all Vikings as Danish and also to regard them as heathen barbarians, whereas in reality they were no less civilized or Christian than the English themselves. Although the Wirral community - and the Thór Stone - derived largely from Norway and not Denmark, somewhat ironically the leader of the "supreme government" by the time the settlements were nearly complete, was Danish - Canute.

# Chapter 16
## CANUTE, ROYAL VISITOR

*"Sea come not hither nor wet the sole of my foot"*

We have already described the connections of Wirral with one of the greatest Norwegian kings – Harald Hárfagri, whose actions were responsible for initiating the Wirral settlements. Seemingly Wirral is also connected with one of the greatest Danish kings – King Canute (Knútur I, 995-1035AD or "Knútur the great"). Canute, full name Knútur Sveinsson, i.e. "son of Sveinn", was king of England from 1016, Denmark from 1019 and also much of Norway from 1028 (via his overlord Earl Hákon) until his death on 12 November 1035, after which he was suceeded by his sons Harald (died 1040) and Hardacanute (died 1042). Canute and Harald are both buried at Winchester Cathedral.

The story – legendary or otherwise - of Canute having sat on a chair at a sea-shore and commanding the sea back is well known to many and is certainly not exclusive to Wirral folk[14]. However people from North Wirral genuinely believe that Canute made this attempt somewhere between Meols and Moreton or Leasowe. *"Sea come not hither nor wet the sole of my foot"* was inscribed on the back of the so-called Canute chair which was once on the sea-front at Leasowe Castle before being destroyed by vandals and used as firewood, as recorded in a letter from Ellison. This letter stated the following: "N.F. Ellison seated on chair 1923. The chair was then situated on the sea-wall of the castle by the entrance

---

[14] Contrary to popular belief, Canute did NOT think he could turn the tide back: he staged the charade on the seashore as a parable for his arrogant courtiers, to show that only God had power over the sea and over them - including kings and courtiers. Source: *Vikings!* by Magnus Magnusson, pages 275-6

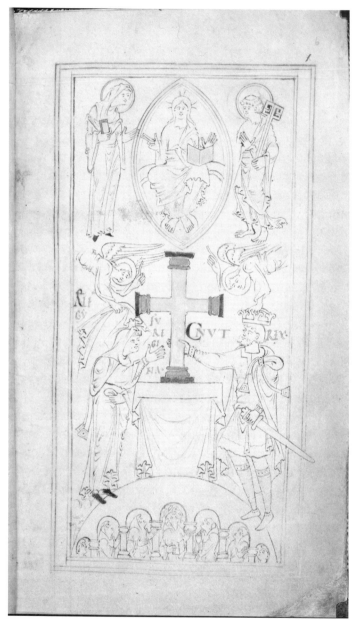

King Canute, with his wife *Aelfgifu*. Page from the *Liber Vitae* of Winchester Cathedral. Courtesy of the British Library, London

gates to the sea. On the back was carved: SEA COME NOT HITHER NOR WET THE SOLE OF MY FOOT. Vandals partly destroyed the chair and when I made enquiries at the castle when I was gathering information for my Wirral book, I was shown at the boiler house a remnant. The chair had been chopped up to fire the boiler. This would be in 1950".

Not having been born until 1955, I just missed the chance to sit on this myself, although my father as a youngster had taken the opportunity.

A similar fate of destruction had earlier befallen a Norse cross in Wallasey Village, which was apparently "a monolith standing twelve feet high and covered with curious cuttings" and was destroyed by vandals in the seventeenth century: the interested reader can read the chapter by J. Bu'Lock in *Wirral and its Viking Heritage.*

The particular chair featured in the figure probably derived from the Cust family in the early Victorian period. Sir Edward Cust K.C.B. from Belton, Lincolnshire, married the owner of Leasowe Castle, Mary Anne Boode, in or sometime near the year 1821. The Cust family no doubt would have promoted the legend itself, although the legendary story should not be dismissed too easily: If King Canute had indeed visited the North Wirral shore in this way he would have found this a very supportive part of his kingdom in an area thickly populated by Scandinavians – albeit Norwegians not Danes. Canute at the time would have been one of the most powerful figures at the start of the 2nd millenium, being King of both Denmark and England.

Legend – as it almost certainly was – or not, King Canute was highly significant for the Wirralonian in that his rule provided the ideal environment for the Scandinavian community in the Wirral to grow and flourish. His rule saw an expansion of the Scandinavian control of manors and also the Scandinavian grip on the financial affairs of the region, with women playing a prominent role, as we shall now see.

King Canute's chair at Leasowe with N.F."Nomad" Ellison. The inscription "Sea come not hither nor wet the sole of my foot" can just be seen. Photograph courtesy of Frank Biddle, local expert on Moreton, Wirral

CANUTE'S CHAIR
LEASOWE CASTLE

N F Ellison seated on Chair 1923
The chair was then situated on the
sea-wall of the Castle by the entrance
gates to the sea. On the back was
carved

SEA COME NOT HITHER NOR WET
THE SOLE OF MY FOOT
Vandals partly destroyed the chair
& when I made enquiries at the Castle
when I was gathering information
for my Wirral book, I was shown in
the boiler-house, a remnant. The
had been chopped up to fire the boiler.
This would be in 1950

J Y Ellison

Ellison's letter. Photograph courtesy of Frank Biddle

185

# Chapter 17
## SIGRÍÐR: LADY OF WALLASEY

*"I, Robert son of Robert of Wallasey .... assign a half a selion which is called Seurydzis alfland."* Robert of Wallasey, Charter of 1280.

This quotation translated from Latin from a 13th century charter (now stored in the John Rylands Library, Manchester) is from Robert of Wallasey, descendant of a Norman Baron. The particular "half selion" or "alfland" (halfland) which he is kindly passing on to someone else once belonged to the Norse lady *Sigríðr* (and who he refers to as "Seurydzis"). The charter also identifies the nearby "le Schepe Rake" (Sheep lane) and "le Rake" (The Lane), as well as le Skere (the Skerry, ON sker) in Wallasey, the latter as Alexander Samson's fishery. The complete translation of this Charter is given in *Wirral and its Viking Heritage*.

Although the land named after her remained, it is likely that *Sigríðr* had long since gone by the time the 1280 Charter was written. It is however reassuring that at some stage between the Viking colonisation and the writing of the Charter she was a landowner, thus supporting the view that women played a prominent role in the Wirral Norse administration. We make further comment about this below.

Her name - or that of another *Sigríðr* - also appears in the list of pre-Domesday moneyers (see also below) and also in the list of the many Norse landowners in the Wirral and surrounds:

Arngrímr (recorded in Domesday Book as Haregrim, Aregrim)
Árni (Erne, Erni) - possible the same Árni of The Arno in Oxton (see Chapter 8)

Original Latin Transcript (from 1280) identifying Sigríðr (as *Seurydzis*) as well as the *le Schepe Rake*, *le Rake* and *le Skere* in Wallasey. This transcript is now in the John Rylands Library, Manchester (catalogue number: JRC*1482*)

Let it be known to all people both present and future that I, Robert son of Robert of Wallasey, have given, granted and by this present my charter have confirmed to Philip of Benfield and his heirs or assigns one bovate of land with appurtenances out of my demesne in the vill of Kirby in Wallasey, namely the bovate which Thomas Gallicus held in the same vill of the gift of lady Alina, and also twelve selions of land with the third part of one selion which extends to Hole siche between the selion of Luke of Bidston and the selion of Alexander Samson, that is to say those selions with the third part of the said selion which William Welsh of Hooton previously held of me to farm in the same vill, and two and a half selions of land of which one is called le Schepe Rake and the other le Blodgreveland, extending as far as le Rake, and the half-selion which is called Seurydzis Alfland, and one selion of land with calf(?) lying between the church land and the land of William Samson, with a certain fishery upon Hoylake lying between the former fishery of Alexander Samson and le Skere...

Translation of the John Rylands Charter *1482* (dated 1280) up to *"le Skere"*...
Translation and comments (in brackets) by Paul Cavill

189

# Ingimund's Saga

Arnkell (Archil)
Ásgautr (Ansgot, Osgot) – of Hargrave Hall (Chapter 10)
Beollán* (Belam)
Björnúlfr (Bernulf)
Brunn (Brun)
Frani (Fran)
Gamall (Gamel)
Grímkell (Grinchel)
Grímr (Grim)
Gunningr (Gunninc)
Gunnarr (Gunner)
Gunnvör (Gunnor)
Guðleikr (Gotlac)
Hákon (Hacon, Hacun)
Hókun
Hálfdan (Halden, Alden)
Hásteinn (Hasten)
Hrafn (Rauen)
Hrafnkell (Rauechel, Rauenchel, Rauecate)
Hrafnsvartr (Rauesuar, Rausue)
Hundingr (Hundingr, Hundin)
Hundólfr (Hundulf)
Karl, Karli (Carle)
Ketill (Chetel)
Kolbeinn (Colben)
Loðinn (Loten)
Morfari* (Morfar)
Ormr (Orme)
Ragnaldr (Ragenal)
**Sigríðr** (Segrid)
Steinkell (Steinchetel)
Steinn (Stein)
Steinólfr (Stenulf)
Tóki (Tochi)
Úlfkell (Ulchel, Ulchetel)
Úlfr (Ulf)
Vetriðr (Wintrelet)
Þjoðólfr (Dedol, Dedou)
Þórðr (Toret, Toreth)

To this list of known Norsemen (and women!) we can add the following list of moneyers also recorded:

Fargrímr (Fargrim)
Kolbeinn (recorded in Domesday as Colben)
Kolbrandr (Coalbrand)
Krókr (Croc)
Húskarl (Huscarl)
Svartkollr (Sweartcol)
Svertingr (Swertinc)
Sveinn (Swegen)
Þóraldr (Thorald)
Þormóðr (Thurmod)

In the Century after 1066 the following moneyers also appear:

Hrafnsvartr (Ravenswart)
Hundólfr (Unnulf)
Sunnúlfr (Sunoulf)
Þorbjörn (Thurbern)

The following moneyers bearing names of Irish origin are also recorded, about which the historian F.T. Wainwright says the following: "there can be no doubt that the Norsemen who introduced these names had long lived in Ireland; perhaps also the Scandinavian hordes which settled in Wirral included many native Irish adventurers, as indeed is suggested by the Three Fragments"

Mældomen and Mælsuthan (10th Century)
Macthusan (11th Century – during the reign of King Canute)
Gillichrist (11th Century – King Harald I and King Hardacanute)
Gillemor (12th Century - Henry I)

Wainwright also noted that Scandinavian personal names continued in existence long after the Norman conquest. Although no collection is available, one frequently meets Scandinavian names in medieval documents. In the Chester

Chartulary are found names of men like Anketill, Anschetill, Asschetill (ON *Áskell, Ásketill*), John Gamel (ON *Gamall*), Rauen (ON *Hrafn*), Orm (ON *Ormr*), Osgot (ON *Ásgautr*), Steinolf (ON *Steinólfr*), Sweinn (ON *Sveinn*) and Toki (ON *Tóki*), and the women's names Gunwara (ON *Gunnvör*) and Gutha (ON *Gyða*, the same as Harald Hárfagri's wife - Chapter 3). All these names belong to the 12th and 13th centuries and they show that the Scandinavian influence on personal nomenclature was neither slight nor transient. One may also suppose that if Scandinavian names were still in use in the 13th Century then a Scandinavian language was still being spoken by the locals.

To this list of recorded Norsemen we can add those whose names have been forever embedded in Wirral place names (Chapters 5-7). The following are recorded in names inside the border of the main Wirral Norse enclave:

Árni (Arno Hill, The Arno in Oxton Parish)
Gunnhildr (Gonnille Pool in Tranmere)
Karli (Calthorpe in Bidston)
Ketill (Kettle Well Garden in Wallasey)
Ragnhildr (Raynilde's Pool in Tranmere)
**Sigríðr** (Sigriðr's Halfland in Wallasey)
Steinkell (Steyncolesdale in Thurstaston)
Sveinn (Sven Tor in Heswall)
Tóki (Toki's ford in Wallasey)
Úfaldi (Ufilys brow in Saughall Massie)
Úfaldi (Vfeldesgrene -Birkenhead Park)
Þorsteinn (Thurstaston)

and the following in outliers, still in Wirral but outside the main Norse enclave:

Fiðill (Fiddlestone in Burton Parish)
Grímr (Grymisgreue in Woodbank)

Ingríðr (Ingriessiche - Ingríðr's stream in Capenhurst)
Ketill (Ketilspol - Riveacre park in Hooton)
Ragnaldr (Rawnuesfeld in Whitby)
Þóraldr (Mollington-Torrold, now Mollington)

We can at last attempt to connect these "place name" people
with the lists of landowners and moneyers above. Surprisingly
it seems that neither *Þorsteinn* who gives his name to
Thurstaston nor *Úfaldi* of Birkenhead Park are recorded as
landowners or moneyers although the following stand out:
*Árni* of Oxton, *Karli* of Bidston, *Ketill* of Wallasey and/or
Hooton, *Ragnaldr* of Whitby, *Steinkell* of Thurstaston, *Tóki* of
Wallasey, *Grímr* of Woodbank, *Þóraldr* of Mollington and
finally our *Sigríðr*.

**Women in the Wirral Norse Society**
Almost a quarter of the Norse people giving their names to
places in the Wirral are women: the role of women was
important throughout the Norwegian commonwealth. Three
Icelandic sagas in particular bring out the importance of
women in Norse society: *Laxdæla Saga, Njál's Saga, and
Eirík's Saga* (The Saga of Eirík the Red). The latter refers
extensively to the Icelandic woman Guðríður Þorbjarnardóttir
("Guðríður, daughter of Þorbjörn") a Christian convert who
was famous as a pioneer in the New World, a pilgrim to Rome
and a virtuous mum! Kristín Bragadóttir and Patrick J. Stevens
writing in *Stefnumót við Íslenska Sagnahefð* (Living and
Reliving the Icelandic Sagas):

"The women of the North played a fairly traditional role in
society, as the rigours of childbearing and domestic life
defined their lives. Nonetheless, Germanic law generally
accorded Nordic women certain rights that most (other)
European women did not enjoy. Pre-Christian Icelandic

women could seek divorce as well as refuse betrothal. Icelandic women had property rights; both the wife and mistress of Snorri Sturluson were women of considerable wealth".

This would be appear to be the case of the Tranmere women *Gunnhildr* and *Ragnhildr*, *Ingríðr* of Capenhurst and also *Sigríðr* – Lady of Wallasey.

# CHAPTER 18

# LOST AND FOUND:

# SCOUSE AND SKAUS

And so ends our story of Wirral and its Vikings – 1100 years sounds a long time since their first arrival with Ingimund - but it is only 40 generations ago. Although the Scandinavian language – Old Norse – was spoken as late as the 13th Century it has now long since gone … well almost: it remains in a way most people don't realise. The local dialect – "*Scouse*" – even in its "posh" form - with its characteristic pitch variation is a direct pass down from the Wirral Norse and comes from a time when Liverpool as a place had hardly got going and indeed was very much a satellite of the main Wirral community. It was therefore of some irony that, centuries later, when Liverpool had become a major seaport, Norwegian sailors walking the docks, introduced the stewy dish called Labskaus or "Scouse" to the community, from which the term "Scouser" arose to describe the locals. Perhaps Wirralonians and not Liverpudlians are the true Scousers or *Skausers*!

**Window on the world**

The Old Norse language has also left its mark in modern English language – as a simple example, if you ask for an egg in a shop you are speaking Norse. Modern Norwegian has also developed away from the Old Norse language, although it too is still closely related to English. For example English and Norwegian  (and also Danish) are the only languages which have the same basic word for window (Norwegian – *vindu*): Swedish seems to take the German form (fenster) and in Icelandic it is *gluggi*! The root behind both window and vindu is is *vind-augr* "wind-eye".

*Ingimund's Saga*

## Finding the old language of the Wirral-Norse

The old Viking language of Old Norse – or something very close to it – is still spoken today in Iceland. Modern Icelandic has changed very little since the Norsemen arrived there in the 9th century. Those wanting to learn a few phrases can do this by downloading the many helpful pages on the WEB such as http://astro.ocis.temple.edu/~feeley/icetrans.html. The keen person can learn more from, for example, P.J.T. Glendening's *Icelandic* in the Hodder and Stoughton's Teach Yourself Books series, and even more from, for example, the excellent *Linguaphone - Icelandic* productions. Modern Norwegian is also covered by both Teach Yourself Books and Linguaphone productions. A selected bibliography follows this final Chapter.

## Postscript

To finish it is worth quoting the remarks of Samuel Laing, a 19th Century translator of Snorri Sturluson's *Heimskringla* "Sagas of the Norse kings" in his Translators Preface:

"These Northmen have not merely been the forefathers of the people, but of the institutions and character of the nation, to an extent not sufficiently considered by our historians. Civilised or not in comparison with the Anglo-Saxons, the Northmen must have left their influences of their character, institutions, barbarism or culture, among their own posterity. They occupied one third of all England for many generations, under their own laws; and for half a century nearly, immediately previous to the Norman conquerors, they held the supreme government of the country."

Perhaps nowhere else do these sentiments apply more to than the Wirral. It is hoped that this book and its companion – *Wirral and its Viking Heritage* – a comprehensive edited collection of essays - will revive this largely lost tradition.

# FURTHER READING

## MAIN

Cavill, P., Harding, S.E. and Jesch, J. (2000) *Wirral and its Viking Heritage,* English Place-Names Society, Nottingham, U.K.
A comprehensive companion to the present book. Includes also contributions from S. Bean and A. Wawn and classical essays from the late J.D. Bu'Lock, F.T. Wainwright, W.G. Collingwood and J. McNeal Dodgson.

## GENERAL

*(N.B. Following convention, Icelandic authors are given first name first)*

Anderson, A. (1964) *The Story of Bromborough* (locally published: copies in the local library at Bromborough)

Biddle, F. and Fellowes, A. (1992) *Moreton Wirral: A Pictorial History, Volume 2* (see pages 46 & 53) Countyvise Ltd., Birkenhead U.K.

Chitty, G. *Wirral Rural Fringes Survey.* Journal of the Merseyside Archaeological Society, 2, 1-22 (1978). The archaeological finding at Bromborough Court is reported as "A Further Note" on p81.

Cohat, Y. (1992) *The Vikings - Lords of the Seas,* Translated by Ruth Daniel, Thames and Hudson Ltd., London, U.K.

Dawson, G. (1998) *Wirral Gleanings,* Dawson Publishing, Irby U.K.
Includes Warmby, the "well" and Scarbrook Hill at Heswall

Dawson, G. (1992) *Tingvelle: A History of Thingwall and other North Wirral farming villages* (see page 2), Dawson Publishing, Irby U.K.

Dodgson, J. McN. (1972) *The Place-Names of Cheshire Part IV,* English Place-Name Society Vol. 47., Cambridge University Press, Cambridge U.K
Comprehensive list of Cheshire Place Names. Part IV deals with Wirral

Ellison, N.F. (1955) *The Wirral Peninsula*, Redwood Burn Ltd., Trowbridge & Esher, U.K.

Fellows-Jensen, G. (1992) Scandinavian Place-Names of the Irish Sea Province. In (Graham-Campbell, J., editor) *Viking Treasure from the North West*, page 39, National Museums and Galleries on Merseyside Occasional Papers, Liverpool Museum Number 5, Liverpool, UK

Glendening, P.J.T. (1961) *Icelandic* (1961) Hodder and Stoughton, London, U.K.
Modern Icelandic is very similar to the language spoken by the Wirral Norse people.

Gordon, E.V. (1957) *Introduction to Old Norse.* 2nd edition, revised by A.R. Taylor, Oxford University Press, Oxford U.K.
For those who are particularly interested in the historical aspects of the language

Graham-Campbell, J. ed. (1992) *Viking Treasure from the North West. The Cuerdale Hoard in its Context.* Liverpool Museum, Liverpool, U.K.
Excellent collection of papers by J. Graham-Campbell, M.M. Archibald, N.J. Higham, G. Fellows-Jensen, B.J.N. Edwards, D.

*Further Reading*

Griffiths, S.E. Kruse, D.M. Metcalf, covering a range of topics including Viking treasure and coinage, place-names, archaeology, and coastal trading ports.

Griffiths, D. (1992) The Coastal Trading Ports of the Irish Sea. In (Graham-Campbell, J., editor) *Viking Treasures from the North West. The Cuerdale Hoard in its Context* (pages 63-72). National Museums and Galleries on Merseyside, Liverpool U.K. Excellent article, particularly about Meols. The border/boundary defining the main Wirral Norse enclave is defined.

Haugen, E. (1976) *The Scandinavian Languages.* London

Higham, N.J. (1993) *The Origins of Cheshire.* Manchester University Press, Manchester U.K.

Jochens, J. (1995) *Women in Old Norse Society*, Cornell University Press, Ithaca, New York. U.S.A.

Kristín Bragadóttir and Stevens, P.J. (2000) Living and Reliving the Icelandic Sagas *Stefnumót við Íslenska Sagnahefð*, Landsbóksafn Íslands – Háskólabókasafn, The Library of Congress, Cornell University Library USA, The University of Manitoba Libraries, Canada.
Gives an excellent background to the basis of the Norse-Icelandic sagas and also a good summary of what it was once like in an Old-Norse society.

Krogh, C. (1900) *Snorri Sturluson.* Kongesagaer, Kristiana, Norway

Laura Goodman Salverson (1923) *The Viking Heart*, Toronto, Canada

# Ingimund's Saga

Magnus Magnusson (1976) *Hammer of the North*. Orbis Publishing Limited, London

Magnus Magnusson (1973) *Viking Expansion Westwards*, Bodley Head, London
Seminal work including Viking Archaeology

Magnus Magnusson (1980) *Vikings!* Elsevier-Dutton Pub. Co., Amsterdam, Holland/London. U.K./New York, USA. Second Edition. 2000 (Harvill Press)
My favourite!

Magnus Magnusson and Hermann Pálsson (translators, 1965) *The Vínland Sagas. The Norse Discovery of America*. Penguin Classics, Harmondsworth, U.K.
Includes the Greenland and Eirik's Sagas

Magnus Magnusson and Hermann Pálsson (translators, 1966) *King Harald's Saga*. Penguin Classics, Hammondsworth: Penguin.

Meehan, A. (1996) *The Dragon and the Griffin: The Viking Impact.* Thames and Hudson, London.
Scandinavian styles in Celtic art

Omerod G. (1882) *The History of the County Palatine and City of Chester.* 2nd edition revised by Thomas Helsby. George Routledge & Sons, London.
Dated but still useful

Orchard, A. (1997) *Dictionary of Norse Myth and Legend*. Cassel, London U.K.

Snorri Sturluson *Heimskringla: Sagas of the Norse Kings*. Translated by S. Laing, revised with footnotes P. Foote. (1961)

Everyman's Library, Dent (London, U.K.) and Dutton (New York U.S.A.).
History of the Kings of Norway from the early 6th to the late 12th Centuries. Of particular interest to the Wirral is Chapter 3 (Harald Hárfagri) and Chapter 8 (Ólaf the Saint).

Snorri Sturluson    *Egils Saga* : Translated and edited by Christine Fell and includes peoms by John Lucas (1975) Everyman's Library, Dent (London, U.K.) and Dutton (New York U.S.A.)
Includes Harald Hárfagri and a little on *Brunanburh*

Snorri Sturluson *The Poetic Edda*. Translated by Carolyn Larrington (1996). Oxford University Press, Oxford U.K.

Snorri Sturluson *The Prose Edda: Tales from Norse Mythology*. Translated by Jean I Young (1954). Bowes and Bowes (Cambridge) and University of California Press (Berkeley, Los Angeles and London).
Stories of Thór and the other Norse gods

Thacker, A.T. (1987) *Scandinavian Settlements in Cheshire*. In The Victoria History of the County of Chester vol I, eds B.E. Harris and A.T. Thacker, p254-260, Oxford University Press, Oxford, U.K.

Wainwright, F.T. *Scandinavian England*. Edited by H.P.R. Finsberg, Philimore Press, Chichester
The book is dominated by the Wirral, although the key articles have been reproduced in "Wirral and its Viking Heritage" above.

*Ingimund's Saga*

## ARTICLES FROM THE JOURNAL OF THE
## ENGLISH PLACE NAMES SOCIETY (JEPNS)

The following articles have recently appeared which are worth reading
Coates, R. 'Liscard and Irish names in Northern Wirral', JEPNS vol. 30 (1997-8), pages 23-6
Gelling, M. 'Paganism and Christianity in Wirral?' JEPNS vol 25 (1992-3), page 11

## BOOKS FOR CHILDREN

Chrisp, P. (1999) *On the Trail of the Vikings in Britain*, Franklin Watts, New York, London & Sydney
Includes the Things

Friel, M. (1994) *Distant Voices*, Poolbeg, Dublin
Childrens fiction book about Vikings in Dublin

Ganeri, A. (1997) *All in a Day's Work - Raiders and Traders: The Vikings*, Heinemann
All aspects of Viking Life

Simpson, J. (1967) *Everyday Life in the Viking Age,* Carousel Books, London

## FILMS

Magnus Magnusson (1980): BBC series "Vikings!":
Hammer of the North
Bolt from the Blue
England at Bay

Bitter Is the Wind
From the Fury of the Northmen
An Island Called Thule
The Empire of the Northern Shores
Here King Harold Is Killed
Hálfdan Was Here
The Ultimate Outpost
The Vínland Mystery

Screenplay: "The Norseman" (Panavision, 1978)
One of the better Viking fiction films, starring Lee Majors - Norse discovery of America and their encounters with the native peoples.

## AUDIO TAPE

Magnus Magnusson (1985): Tales from Viking Times/BBC Audio Cassettes/7083

## WEB PAGES

Hnefatafl – history of the game from 400AD
http://www.realtime.com/~gunnora/games.htm

Hnefatafl: play the Viking board game!:
http://www.expomedia.se/tablut/eng/history.htm

Harald Hárfagri:
http://www.sawyer-family.org/d0035/I15104.html
http://www.alaska.net/~aulbach/Fairhair.HTML

Icelandic Language:
http://astro.ocis.temple.edu/~feeley/icetrans.html

Martin Tranmæl Web page:
http://home.sol.no/~jbrenna/skole/tranm%e61.html
http://www.lysator.liu.se/runeberg/authors/tranmmar.html
Norwegian dictionary:
http://www.dokpro.uio.no/ordboksoek.html

Olave/ Ólaf the Saint:
http://viking.no/e/people/st.olav/e-olav.htm.

St. Bridget, joint patron saint of Ireland:
http://catholic.org/saints/saints/brigidireland.html.

The Viking Network Bibliography - good comprehensive list
of books
http://viking.no/vnet/info/e-bibliography.htm

Time Line of Viking History
http:/www.mtsu.edu/~kgregg/dmir/new/timeline.html

Trani (crane bird) web page:
http://europa.eu.int/comm/environment/nature/directive/gru
s_grus.htm

# Index

# Index

# WONDERFUL WIRRAL

## Surprise Peninsula in the North West

D. Turner

### A great day out for all the family the Visitor Attractions include:

Port Sunlight Village • Historic Warships • Mersey Ferries • Birkenhead Tramways
Ness Botanic Gardens • Europa Pools • Voirrey Embroidery & Brimstage Hall
Wirral Museums • West Kirby Marine Lake • Max Spielmann Photo Visitor Centre
Birkenhead Heritage Trail • Wirral Country Park

For further details contact the Tourist Information Centre.
Woodside Ferry Booking Hall, Birkenhead, Wirral  CH41 6DU  Tel: 0151 647 6780

**The Wirral Consortium
of Visitor Attractions**

National Centre for
Molecular Hydrodynamics

A biological macromolecule moves faster through water than a Viking ship.... well, relatively speaking!

Water movement technologies, or "Hydrodynamics" provide a powerful way of understanding how the large molecules of nature behave and interact in what for many, is their natural environment - water - just like a Viking!

The National Centre for Molecular Hydrodynamics provides an international North-European Facility for their study, and via its Business Centre a Service for the Biotechnology, Pharmaceutical and Food Industries. It also offers a one year training course for Science Graduates - the MSc in Applied Biomolecular Technology.

Contact: Steve Harding, NCMH, University of Nottingham, School of Biosciences, Sutton Bonington LE12 5RD UK

email: Steve.Harding@nottingham.ac.uk,
fax: +44 115 951 6148.
Find us on: http://www.nottingham.ac.uk/

Mældomen, 112, 191
Mælsuthan, 191
MacEgan, N, 7
MacFirbis, D, 7
Mackel Brock, 105
Magnus Magnusson, 81, 181
Magnus the Good, King of Norway, 142
Mainwaring estate, 83, 132
Mainwaring map, 132
Malmesbury, William of, 122, 128
Mark Rake, 74
Marled Thwaite
Marshland, 29
Marshy, 27
Matthews, Godfrey, 128
Meadow Thwaite, 48
Mecca Brook, 55, 101
Meckansedge, 76
Melar, 39
Mellons, 50
Melr, 1, 2, 3
Meols, 1, 3, 29, 36, 38, 39, 137, 181
Mercians, 13, 123
Meresige, 129
Mereston, 116
Mersey river, estuary, 21, 121, 125, 137, 142
Merseyside Conservation Centre, 154
Meynwarin, Warrin de, 115
Mickansedge, 60
Mickell Brook, 80
Mickeldale, 96, 115, 116
Mickenbrook, 105
Mickledale, 24, 66, 116-119
Mickle Moor Meadow, 66
Mickwell, 92
Mickwell Brow, 92
Mickwell, Covert, 92
Middle Rake Hey, 56
Midlethrinlowe, 116
Mill Lane, 24, 118
Milner Copse, 30, 59

Milner Road, 30, 57, 59
Mini-state, Wirral-Norse, 36
Mjöllnir, Thór's Hammer, 10, 38, 170-179
Mockbeggar Wharf, 137
Mollington-Torrold, 41, 193
Moore Flat, 85
Mop-Hair, 18
Moreton, 29, 41, 63, 181
Moreton cum Lingham, 29, 41, 63
Moreton Flatt, 68
Morfari, 190
Morris Dancers, Dancing, 175, 176
Moster Thing, 150
Mót, 145
Mount Road, Bebington, 136

Near Carr Bridge Field, 61
Near Flatt, 67
Near Holmes Wood, 53
Near Intake, 95
Near Rake Hay, 54
Near Storeton Field, 77
Nearer Bridgets, 8
Nehemias MacEgan, 7
Ness, 41, 92
Ness Acre, 96
Ness Croft, 96
Neston, 21, 24, 26, 29, 41
New Carr, 73
New Ferry, 91
New Home, 70
New Larton Hay, 55
New Rake Hey, 95
Newton, 29, 66, 99, 105
Newton Breken, 66
Newton Car, 66
Newton Rake, 67, 105
Nicolle, Serge, 2
Niðaros (Trondheim), 18
Njál's saga, 193
Noctorum, 8, 41, 67
Norris, Thomas, 102

# THE CITY OF TRONDHEIM WELCOMES YOU!

Trondheim: The west wall of the Medieval Nidaros Cathedral.

**TRONDHEIM has over a thousand years of experience in receiving visitors....** In the Middle Ages, the city was one of the most visited pilgrimage destinations in the whole of Europe: St. Olav, the man who played a leading role in bringing Christianity to Scandinavia and Northern Europe, is buried here. It was a far-sighted and fortunate decision that the Viking King Olav Tryggvason made when he founded the city of Trondheim (Nidaros) in 997 AD. Today, Trondheim is the third largest city in Norway, and it holds a special place in the country's history and culture. Here the past and present live side by side in a particularly harmonious fellowship...

TRONDHEIM AKTIVUM AS
VISITORS AND CONVENTION BUREAU
Tel: + 47 73 80 76 60
Fax:  + 47 73 80 76 70
www.trondheim.com

Index

Ulfhildr, 113
Úlfkell, 190
Unarheimr, Norway, 145
Unarheimr Thing, 144
Upper Flat, 74
Uppsala, 16
Upton, 29, 68, 78
Utterthwaite, 48, 100

Valders, 16
Valhalla, Hall of the Norse gods, 1,
150
Valholl, 1
Vertriðr, 190
Vestfold, 16
Vestri-kirkjubær, 27, 39
Vestri Kirkjubyr, 3, 27
Vfeldesgrene, Claughton, 54, 162,
192
Viborg Thing, Denmark, 144
Victorians, 171, 175, 177, 178
Vilkynstane, 116-118
Vind-augr, "Wind-eye", 195
Vínheiði, 122
Vínheiði við Vínuskógar, 125
Vinland, 19

Wagner, Gustav (German compos-
er), 171
Wainwright, F.T., 1, 8, 21, 191
Waley-Carr, 79
Wallacre, 48
Wallacre Road, 79
Wall Rake, 58
Wallasey, 27, 29, 78, 128,132, 151,
166-168, 192, 193
Wallasey Charter, 11
Wallasey Grammar School, 29, 64
Wallasey Pool, 137, 143
Wallasey School, 29
Wallasey Village, 1, 38, 41, 150, 183
Wargraves, 83, 132
Warmby, 27, 28, 58
Warmby Lane, 58

Web Sites, 11
Wednesday, 174
Welsh, 36
Welsh Chronicles, 7
Wessex, 124
West Car, 64
West Carr Hay, 64
West Carr Meadow, 64
West Kirby, 3, 27, 28, 30, 38, 39, 41,
80, 99, 105, 113,148, 150-157
West Saxons, 123
Westfold, 16
Whartons Arrowe, 45
Whinney Thwaite, 100
Whinney's Thwaite, 48
Whitby, Wirral, 27-30, 80, 105, 113,
142, 193
Whitby's Acre, 88
Whitbytylth, 88
Whitmore, William, 102, 103
Widings Arrowe, 45
Willaston, 26, 29, 95, 115, 118, 161
Willow Valley, 160
Wimbricks, 56, 73
Winchester Cathedral, 181, 182
Window, 194
Winge, Martin (Swedish artist), 172
Winthrop, 53
Wirral and its Viking Heritage,
book, 8, 30, 36, 154, 183, 187, 196
Wirral Charters, 24
Wirral Metropolitan Borough, 26
Wirral Parishes, 21, 22
Wodekirkja (Woodchurch), 41, 150
Wolfeld's Gate, 103
Women, prominence in Norse
Society, 187, 193-194
Wood Clints, 84
Woodbank, 30, 96, 163, 192
Woodchurch, 41, 80 150
Wranglandes, 52, 101, 104
Wrangol, 52
Wro, The, 52, 101
Wyhon Flatt, 55

A Companion Volume to *Ingimund's Saga*

# Wirral and its Viking Heritage

by
Paul Cavill, Stephen E. Harding and Judith Jesch

This book is a guide to the Viking impact on Wirral. it includes reprinted illustrated essays from F.T. Wainwright, John McN. Dodgson, J.D.Bu'lock and W.G. Collingwood, on the history, art and names of the region. The work is brought up to date by original contributions from Simon C. Bean, Stephen E. Harding, Judith Jesch and Andrew Wawn on recent developments in the history, archaeology, scholarly and popular interest in the Wirral. It is completed by a gazetteer examining the origins of the major names, which also forms an index to the volume.

The book provides absorbing reading and is an important resource for anyone interested in the past of the Wirral and the origins of its names.

### Published by the English Place-Name Society

School of English Studies, University of Nottingham, Nottingham NG7 2RD.
Tel: 0115 951 5919.    Fax: 0115 951 5924.
Registered Charity No. 257891.

Popular Series, ISBN 0 904889 59 9
Paperback, 235 x 157mm, ix + 149pp

## Price £11.99

If you would like to receive
information about other

## Countyvise
## Local Interest books

please contact us at:

Countyvise Ltd
14 Appin Road
Birkenhead
Merseyside
CH41 9HH

Tel: 0151 647 3333
Fax: 0151 647 8286
email: cv@birkenheadpress.co.uk

We will add your name to our mailing list

Typeset and printed in Wirral by

Birkenhead Press Ltd.
14 Appin Road
Birkenhead
Merseyside
CH41 9HH

Tel: 0151 647 3333
Fax: 0151 647 8286